QUIET SOBRIETY

*An honest story about
how to stop drinking alcohol
when nothing else has worked.*

Ben Mallory

CONTENTS

PART I
THE COLLAPSE BEFORE THE CLIMB

THE MORNING THAT SHOULDN'T HAVE HAPPENED	1
THE LIE HE BELIEVED	10
THE THING HE CAN'T REMEMBER	16
THE MIRROR SCENE	24
THE SILENCE THAT SCREAMED	31

PART II
THE WAR INSIDE

DAY ONE, AGAIN	43
THE HOUR THAT NEVER ENDS	49
THE SUPERMARKET GHOSTS	57
THE FUCK-IT NIGHT	64
THE PHOTO ON THE FRIDGE	71
THE FIRST TIME HE SPOKE	79
THE CLOSED DOOR	85
THE ROOM WHERE HE SLEPT ON THE FLOOR	92

PART III
WHEN NOTHING HAPPENS, BUT EVERYTHING CHANGES

THE 30TH DAY	103

| THE FIRST YES | 111 |
| THE TINY REPAIR | 120 |

PART IV
THE QUIET BECOMING

THE FEAR OF BEING OKAY	129
THE FIRST REAL LAUGH	137
THE SMALLEST BRAVE THING	144

PART V
THE MAN WHO CAME BACK

BRIDGES, NOT APOLOGIES	155
WHAT HE CAME BACK FOR	162
THIS ISN'T THE END. IT'S THE BEGINNING OF SOMEONE ELSE'S STORY — BECAUSE OF YOU	173

PART I
THE COLLAPSE BEFORE THE CLIMB

THE MORNING THAT SHOULDN'T HAVE HAPPENED

Waking Up Wrong

You wake up sideways. Face halfway off the pillow, mouth open, throat scorched like you've been swallowing sandpaper all night. It's not even light out — or maybe it is. The blinds are shut, but a sliver of gray leaks through, just enough to make you flinch.

Your tongue tastes like coins. Your head isn't pounding — it's humming. A low, electric throb behind your eyes. Like your brain's been left in the microwave a few seconds too long.

You roll onto your back. The ceiling swims. The room doesn't feel familiar at first — and that's the part that should scare you. But it doesn't. It's normal now. Waking up not knowing how you got here. Or when.

There's a sock on the lamp. A shirt on the floor. The smell in the air is stale — sweat, booze, something sweet that turned sour. You don't need to look around to know what this is.

This is the wreckage.

The crash you keep waking up inside of.

You blink a few times. Once. Again. Still dark, still heavy. Your limbs feel like they're filled with wet cement. Even breathing takes effort.

And then the first thought hits you. Not a word, not a sentence — just a pulse of panic in your chest.

Something happened.
And you don't remember what.

Your hand searches the nightstand, knocking over a plastic bottle, maybe Advil, maybe vodka. You don't care. Your fingers find the phone — cold, cracked, nearly dead. The screen lights up like it's judging you.

09:43 AM.
Shit.

Work. You had work. You were supposed to be there.

Or maybe it wasn't work. Maybe it was something else. Someone else.

Your stomach flips. Not from the hangover — that's background noise by now — but from the feeling. The knowing. That whatever it was, you've already missed it.

You close your eyes. You open them again. Nothing changes.

The sheets are twisted around your legs. You feel the urge to kick them off, but even that takes more strength than you've got.

You sit up slowly, like your body's warning you not to.

And that's when the second thought hits:

This isn't the first time.
Not even the tenth.

It's just another entry in a long, blurry list of mornings that shouldn't have happened.

Your heart's beating now — not fast, but heavy. Each thump like a knock on a locked door inside your chest. You know what's behind it. Regret. Shame. That voice.

"You said you were done."

"You promised."

"You lied."

You swing your legs over the edge of the bed. The carpet's cold. There's an old stain near your foot — could be coffee, could be worse. You're not investigating.

You stand up.

You almost fall.

Your knees buckle a little. Your balance is off. You grip the wall for support and feel the sweat already starting to bead at the base of your neck.

This is withdrawal. Or punishment. Same thing, really.

You shuffle toward the door.

It creaks when you open it — like even the house is tired of you.

There's a dull ache in your ribs. You press there. No bruise, not yet. Just sore. From sleeping twisted? Or something else?

There's a moment where you pause in the hallway. Your eyes catch the mirror at the end. And you hesitate.

You're not ready to see what's there.
Not yet.

You turn into the bathroom instead. Lights off. You piss in the dark. Your hands shake a little, just enough to notice. You flush. You wash. You splash cold water on your face and hope it wakes something up.

It doesn't.

You flick the switch. The mirror comes alive. And so does the shame.

But that's for later.

Right now, all you can do is stand there. Shirtless. Hollow. Unsteady.

The world is already happening without you. The clock's ticking. People are out there — living, working, calling, texting. Moving forward.

And you?

You're just waking up wrong.

Again.

But your body remembers what you won't admit yet:

This is not rock bottom.
This is routine.

The Phone That Won't Stop

The phone buzzes in your hand. Again. Like it's trying to remind you: there's still a world out there, and you've let it down. Again.

Twelve missed calls.
Three from work — not your boss, but his assistant. The one who still sounds polite, even when she's disappointed.

Two from your ex. That's worse. Because she never calls unless it's about your son.
One from your sister. And somehow… that's the one that stings the most.

The rest are just numbers. A group contact from the meetings. A guy named Chris you barely remember — he once said, "Call me if it gets bad." You never did.

There's a voicemail notification. You stare at it like it's a live wire. You already know what it says. Not the words, but the tone. That quiet ache wrapped in frustration. Disappointment wearing grief like perfume.

You press play.

The voice is familiar — broken in the same places you are. It's her. You brace for the sound.

"I can't do this again, Mike."

Your name lands like a gavel.

"You promised. I let you come over. You looked me in the eye."

There's a pause. A sharp inhale. She's holding something back.

"I wanted to believe you this time."

That last line?
That's the one that cuts.

Because you remember the moment she means. Her standing by the door. You standing too close. Saying things like, *This time's different,"* and *"I've got it handled.*

Lies — but not on purpose.
You meant them. Every single one.

You just didn't *mean* them enough.

The message ends, but the echo stays. You sit on the edge of the bed, still holding the phone like it might crack open and spill out all the things you forgot.

The screen lights up again.

A text from your boss:
Don't bother coming in. We'll talk when you're clear.

Clear.

The word hits harder than it should.

Clear as in sober?
Clear as in fired?
Clear as in out of his life, out of his company, out of the way?

You don't know.
But either way… it's not good.

You scroll back up. Read the missed calls again. Try to will them into meaning something different. But they don't. They never do.

You think about calling someone back.
Just one person.

Your sister?
Your son's mom?
The guy from the group?

But the thought makes your chest tighten. Like if you reach out, it'll make this real. Like admitting it out loud makes the shame solid.

So you don't.

You sit there, still half-dressed in yesterday's clothes, the phone buzzing now and then like a mosquito in your hand — annoying, persistent, impossible to ignore.

And then… silence.

No more calls.
No more buzzes.
No more anyone.

You're alone. Really alone.

And for the first time this morning, you're awake enough to feel it.

Looking in the Mirror Feels Like Lying

You shuffle toward the bathroom like someone heading to court, knowing they're already guilty.
Not for the shower. Not for a shave. You go because you need to see what damage last night did.

You flick on the light.
Too sharp. Too honest.

There you are.
That bloated face.
The eyes that used to have light now just reflect defeat.
Your lips are cracked. Your skin looks like paper soaked in regret.
You stare at your reflection like it owes you an apology.
But all it does is stare back, quietly accusing.

You lean closer to the mirror.
Not to fix anything. There's nothing to fix.
You just want to know if there's *anyone left inside*.

You whisper, but your voice doesn't come out.
Only the mirror hears:

"What the hell happened to you?"

Your breath fogs the glass.
You wipe it clean like it'll wipe away the shame.
It doesn't.

The silence in the bathroom?
It's louder than any fight you've had.
And right now, it's the only thing not lying to you.

Pretending It's Just a Bad Day

You dress like you're going somewhere.
Even if you're not.
Even if the idea of going anywhere feels laughable right now.

Jeans. T-shirt. Hoodie. All clean enough to pass.
You splash water on your face again—more punishment than refreshment.
There's a smell you can't wash off.
It's not just sweat or vodka.
It's shame.

You rehearse excuses out loud.
"Food poisoning."
"No signal."
"Car battery."
Each one thinner than the last.
Each one betraying how many times you've needed one.

You check your phone again.
Still no new messages.
Of course.

You sit at the edge of the bed, hands dangling between your knees.
The clock ticks too loud.

It's already 10:27.
You were supposed to be at work at 9.
You were supposed to be somewhere else in life three years ago.

You pull your hood over your head.
As if fabric could hide the weight in your chest.

You tell yourself:
"It's just a bad day."

But your chest says,
"It's been years."

And your soul says nothing at all.

THE LIE HE BELIEVED

"I Can Handle It"

You've said it so many times, it's almost a prayer now.
"I can handle it."
Spoken like a charm against the unraveling.

You said it when you poured your first drink at 11 a.m. on your day off.
You said it when you bought only *one* bottle, not three.
You said it after that meeting you left early — the one where everyone smelled like guilt and cheap coffee.

You say it now, staring at the text that says *Don't bother coming in.*

Your body says otherwise. Your phone says otherwise.
The silence around you — it screams *liar.*

But inside, some stubborn thread pulls tight:
"I've got this. I can stop. I've done it before."

(You haven't. Not really. Not long enough to count.)

You walk into the kitchen, like a man going to war with his own cabinets.
There's nothing left to drink — not even orange juice.
You slam the door anyway.
Because empty feels better than temptation.

Your mind plays defense:
"It's just stress."
"It's been a rough week."
"Anyone would break under this much pressure."

You open the window. Let air in. Let excuses out.

You grab your coat. Keys. Wallet.

Not to escape — just to prove to yourself you're *still functioning*. Still capable of normal things.

The door clicks behind you.
You step out like you've done nothing wrong.

But deep inside, you know:

This is the lie that's killing you.
And worst of all —
you still believe it.

The Boss's Ultimatum

You check your voicemail again. Not because you missed anything — you just want to hear it one more time.

Your boss's voice isn't angry. That's what makes it worse.

It's calm. Controlled. The kind of voice people use when they've already made peace with walking away.

"Mike… I covered for you last week. I talked to HR. I told them you were sick. Again. But this—this is it. If I don't see you by the end of the day, we're done."

No yelling. No threats. Just the sound of someone giving up on you gently.

You stand in the kitchen holding the phone like it might forgive you if you grip it hard enough.

End of the day.

That's still hours away. Right?

You could clean up. Shower again. Change your shirt. Show up late and say it was traffic. Or food poisoning. Or anything that's not the truth.

You rehearse it in your head:
"Sorry, I've just been going through some things."
"Got stuck dealing with family stuff."
"Didn't sleep well."

You pause. Swallow.

None of it will work.

He's heard it all before. Hell, he probably used to believe it too.

But even patience has a shelf life.

You slide the phone into your pocket and stare at the floor.

You don't have to go in.

You could just… not.

And that thought?
It feels dangerous.
It feels like surrender.

But it also feels… easy.

And lately, easy has been winning.

The Text That Went Unanswered

Your thumb hovers over the screen.

There it is — the last message you never replied to.

Not from your boss. Not from your ex. Not even from your sister.

It's from Chris.

The guy from the group. The one who gave you his number, looked you in the eye, and said, *"Seriously, man. Any time. No pressure. Just... if it gets bad."*

You never answered.

The message is four days old.
Hey brother, just checking in. You good?

That's it. No judgment. No drama. Just someone reaching a hand across the pit.
And you ghosted him.

You scroll up — nothing before it. Just that single act of care landing in a vacuum.

Your finger lingers on the reply bar.

You could write something.
Now. Right now. Just a word: *"Not really."*
Or even a damn emoji. Anything.

But your thumb doesn't move.

Because if you reply, it opens a door.
And if you open that door, the shame walks through first.

And right now, you're not sure you can look anyone in the eye and say the words you need to say:

"I need help."

So you lock the screen.
Toss the phone on the couch like it's hot.
Like it hurt you.

But it didn't.

It just reminded you:
You had a chance. And you let it ring out.

Passing Out Before Promises

You remember standing by the door last night. Kind of.

Her silhouette in the hallway light. The way she didn't move when you spoke. The weight in her eyes.

You said it again. *"I'm done. I swear. No more."*

She didn't smile. She didn't argue.
She just looked at you like someone who's heard the same lullaby too many times to believe in sleep.

And you meant it. At least, in that moment, with just enough clarity left in your bloodstream to string the words together.
You meant it so hard it almost hurt.

But promises made on weak legs and dry mouths don't last.

Especially not when the bottle's still in the cabinet.
Especially not when silence feels like drowning.
Especially not when the shame gets louder than the love.

So you poured one more. Just to sleep.

Only… you didn't sleep. You blacked out.

Again.

Your last memory is the TV flashing something dumb. A laugh track. A blinking screen.
Then — nothing.

And now, the guilt hits harder than the hangover.

Not because you drank.
But because you lied.
Again.

You sit down on the floor, back against the wall, knees pulled up.

The cup from last night is still there. Half-full. Room temperature. A quiet reminder.

You look at it and say nothing.

Because there's nothing left to say.

Only this:
You broke a promise. Not to her. Not to them.
To yourself.
And that's the one you don't know how to fix.

THE THING HE CAN'T REMEMBER

A Message He Doesn't Recall

You don't remember sending anything.
Not a call. Not a text. Not even thinking about it.
But there it is.

A voice memo.
Sent at 1:37 AM.
To her.

Your thumb hovers over the screen like it's holding a weapon. You don't want to press play.
But you do.

Her voice, shaky, almost whispers:

"I got your message last night. I didn't reply because… I didn't know what to say."

You blink. Message? What message?

She continues:

"You said you were alone. That you were scared. That maybe this time it really was the end."

Your breath catches.
You don't remember saying that.

"You said you didn't think anyone cared anymore. That you weren't sure if you cared either."

Your throat tightens.
You check the message log. You did send it.
Thirty-six seconds long. But you can't bring yourself to play it.

What if you said more?
What if you cried?
What if you begged?

You stare at the screen. Heart pounding now.
It's not just a message.
It's a mirror. One that talks back.

Because the truth is —
You do remember.
Not the details. Not the words.
But the feeling.

That moment when the bottle was almost empty.
When the silence got too loud.
When you looked at the wall and didn't see a way through it.

It wasn't a message.
It was a scream.

Only softer.

And now that it's out there —
you can't unsend it.
You can't unsay what your heart said when your mind was gone.

You put the phone down.
Your hands are shaking again.
Not from the booze.
Not even from withdrawal.

But from truth.

You don't remember sending the message.

But your soul does.
It's been trying to send it for years.

Panic in the Gut

It hits you like a sucker punch from the inside.

Not a full panic attack — not yet.
But the kindling's there. The dry wood stacked. The match already struck.
All it needs is one breath the wrong way, and you're gone.

Your stomach twists.
Not nausea — not quite.
More like gravity shifting. Like your insides just realized something your brain tried to block out.

You sit down fast. Floor. Cold. Unforgiving.
Back against the kitchen cabinet.
You try to breathe, but your chest feels locked.
Like someone tied a belt around your lungs and pulled.

Your hands clench into fists without permission.

You tell yourself, "It's just a wave."
But waves crash. Waves drown.

You've been here before.
This is what happens when memory and regret hold hands.

Your thoughts race in circles:

"What else did I do?"
"Who else did I call?"

"What if I drove?"
"What if I said something I can't unsay?"
"What if I was honest?"

That last one is the worst.

Because being honest — even blacked-out honest —
Means the real you is breaking through.
And the real you is scared.

Your shirt sticks to your back with sweat.
Your knees pull tighter to your chest.
You press your palms into your eyes like maybe darkness will help.

It doesn't.

Your body is sounding alarms your mind can't decode.
Fight, flight… freeze.

You freeze.

Because if you move, you might remember more.
And you're not sure you can survive that.

You stay curled on the floor.
Waiting.
Hoping it passes.

It always does.
But never before it takes a piece of you with it.

Silence on the Other End

You finally do it.

You call the number.

Not because you're ready.

Not because you've gathered your strength.
But because the silence is louder than your fear now, and you need something — anything — to interrupt it.

You stare at the contact name:
"Chris – Group"

Your finger hesitates.
One last moment of control before the wheel turns.

Then — tap.
Ringing.

Once.
Twice.
Three times.

You hold your breath like it'll help the call connect faster.

Then — click.

But it's not him.
It's voicemail.

His voice comes through — calm, kind, recorded:
"Hey, it's Chris. You know what to do."

Beep.

Your mouth opens.

But no sound comes out.

You try. You really try.

You even mouth the words first:
"Hey man, it's Mike… I think I messed up again…"

But nothing makes it past your lips.

It's like your shame wrapped around your vocal cords and tightened.

So instead, you breathe into the phone.
A broken, silent apology.

Then — hang up.

You stare at the screen like maybe it'll give you a second chance.
Like maybe the call didn't happen.

But it did.

And now you've said nothing. Again.

You lean your forehead against the wall, the phone still in your hand.

The line may have disconnected —
but the silence?
It's still here.

And this time…
it's not on the other end.
It's in you.

Realizing This Isn't the First Time

You slump onto the edge of your bed, phone face down on the blanket like it betrayed you.
But it didn't.
You did.

You sit there for a minute. Maybe five. Maybe twenty. Time's weird now—elastic. Slippery.

Then it hits you:
This isn't new.

This exact moment — the cold air, the voicemail, the silence, the ache behind your eyes —
You've lived this before.

Not once.
Not twice.
Dozens of times. Maybe more.

Different nights, different bottles, different broken promises.

But always the same aftermath.

You said, "Last time," so many times it stopped meaning anything.

You apologized with eyes half-shut, with words you barely remembered.

You woke up like this. Sat like this. Regretted like this.

You swore:
"I'll fix it,"
"I'll change,"
"I just need one more chance."

But it wasn't just one.

It was a pattern.
A system.
A cycle you pretended was a streak of bad luck instead of what it really is:

Your life.

You walk to the fridge, like maybe cold air will clear your head.

Inside — a takeout container with something brown and soggy, a bottle of ketchup, and a beer. One beer.

You stare at it.

Not with craving.
Not yet.

With recognition.

Because even that — the leftover bottle — it's part of the choreography.

You always leave one. Like a door cracked open.

Just in case.

You close the fridge.
Hard.

And whisper:

"This is who I am now…"

Then you catch yourself.

No.

Not who you *are*.

Who you've *become*.

And maybe… that's not permanent.

But damn if it doesn't feel like it right now.

THE MIRROR SCENE

Closing the Bathroom Door

You close the bathroom door like you're sealing yourself into a vault. Not to hide. Not exactly. More like… containment. Like you're trying to keep something dangerous in.

The light flickers as you flip the switch. Cheap bulb. Or maybe it's just tired of watching this same scene play out every few nights.

The fan hums, loud and useless.

You look at the lock. Twist it. Not for safety. Just so no one walks in — not that anyone would. But still.

You stand there for a second. Just breathing. Just listening to the sound of your own breath echo off tile. It's too loud. Too rhythmic. You wonder if someone else would think you're calm right now. You're not.

Your eyes find the mirror.

You don't look directly. Not yet. You move in sideways, pretending you're grabbing something — your toothbrush, maybe. But it's just stalling.

Eventually, you face it.

There you are.

And there he is — that guy who always shows up when it's too late to undo anything. Eyes swollen. Cheeks hollow. Beard uneven like it's trying to grow out of grief. Shirt stained under the arms. A cut on your knuckle you don't remember getting.

You stare.

The mirror doesn't lie. That's the problem.

Your hand reaches for the sink, steadying you. Like somehow your reflection might tip you over.

You lean in, close enough to see the blood vessels in your eyes. Red. Webbed. Angry. You look tired. Not tired like you need sleep. Tired like you've been running from something for a decade and it finally caught up.

And for a second — just one terrifying second — you wonder if you're even real anymore. If the reflection is just a ghost trying to remind you what you used to be.

You press your palms into the edge of the sink.

The porcelain is cold. Solid. Honest.

You breathe in. Long. Shaky.

And you ask, barely above a whisper:

"What are you doing, man? What the hell are you doing?"

The question doesn't echo, but it doesn't need to.

It lands in your chest like a stone.

The mirror doesn't answer. It never does. But tonight, it doesn't flinch either.

It just... watches.

And for once, you don't look away.

The Look That Cuts Deeper Than Words

You don't remember hearing her come in.
But when you lift your head — she's there.
Standing in the doorway. Not moving. Not blinking.
Just watching you.

No yelling. No tears. No demands.
Just that look.
The one that says,
"I used to love you. I don't know if I still do."

You expect a scream. A lecture. Something to fight against.
But all she does is look. And it's worse.
Because silence doesn't give you a target.
It just holds up a mirror.

You try to speak.
But your throat closes like it's choking on truth.
You try to stand straighter. But your shoulders collapse.
You want to say:
"I'm sorry."
"This isn't me."
"I'll fix it."
But all you manage is a broken breath.

She doesn't flinch.
She just keeps staring at you.
Like someone trying to find the person they used to believe in —
and realizing he's not there.

You look away.
Because that look?
It's not angry. It's not hurt.

It's empty.
And **emptiness always cuts deeper than rage**.

You hear her keys.
The soft jingle as she turns.
And then — the door.
Closing behind her.

Not slamming.
Just... done.

And for the first time today,
your chest actually aches.
Not from withdrawal. Not from guilt.
But from grief.
Because something just left the room —
and it's not coming back.

"Who Even Are You Now?"

You sit on the edge of the tub.

Not because you're tired — though you are — but because standing feels like pretending. And right now, you're too honest for that.

Your elbows rest on your knees. Your hands dangle like they've given up.

The mirror watches from across the room.

And somewhere between your heart and your ribs, a question starts to form — not loud, not sharp. Just steady. Like a drip from a leaky faucet.

"Who even are you now?"

Not the you from high school — the kid who swore he'd never end up like his old man.

Not the you from that first apartment — hopeful, broke, laughing at gas station wine and dreaming out loud.

Not the you from two years ago, still trying, still fighting, still **believing**.

No.

Now you're the guy with the voicemail no one wants to answer.

The guy people whisper about but don't check on.

The guy who wakes up late and lies before noon.

You tilt your head back, stare at the ceiling like it might have answers written in the cracks.

You whisper it again, this time with less anger and more ache:

"Who the hell even are you?"

And the silence?

It answers.

Not in words — but in the weight in your chest. The pit in your gut. The echo of everything you've lost.

You don't cry. You don't scream.

You just sit there.

And let the question hang in the air like smoke from a fire you didn't mean to start.

The Urge to Break the Glass

Your eyes lock with the reflection again.

You don't blink.

You don't move.

You just stare at him — that hollow-eyed, half-dead version of yourself — and something rises in your chest. Slow. Hot. Acidic.

Rage.

But not at the world. Not at her. Not even at the bottle.

At him.
At you.

Because this didn't just happen.
You let it.
Every lie. Every excuse. Every "just one more."
You built this ruin brick by brick, and now you're the one trapped inside.

Your hand twitches on the sink's edge.

There's a toothbrush holder. A metal soap dish. Anything would do.

It would take one second.
One sharp swing.
One loud crack.

The glass would shatter, and maybe — **maybe** — so would the illusion.
Maybe you could destroy what you've become by destroying the thing that reflects it.

You lift your hand just slightly.

Test the weight of the thought.

But you don't move.

Because deep down, you know…

Breaking the mirror won't change the truth.

It'll only give you something else to clean up.

And you're already drowning in the mess.

You lower your hand.

Grip the counter until your knuckles go white.

And for the first time in a long time, you let yourself feel it — all of it.

The anger.

The shame.

The loss.

The fight you've been dodging.

And the flicker — faint but real — of the man you **might still be**, somewhere under the wreckage.

THE SILENCE THAT SCREAMED

A Child's Eyes, Not Words

You don't hear him come in.

It's the softest sound — a door creaking just enough to let in a child-sized shadow. You're still in the hallway, one hand on the bathroom sink, the other limp at your side. You don't move.

But you feel it.

That presence behind you.

You turn, slow. Like you're afraid to spook him.
Or yourself.

He's standing near the doorway. Small. Still.
Backpack halfway off one shoulder. Hoodie sleeves pulled over his hands.

And the look on his face?

It's not fear. Not confusion.

It's worse.

It's knowing.

Knowing too much for his age.
Knowing this isn't just "a bad day" for Dad.

Knowing the way kids know things no one ever says out loud.

You open your mouth.

But there's nothing.

Not because you can't speak — but because you don't know what would even help.
He doesn't need an explanation.

He's seen the bottles.
He's heard the late-night shouting.
He's watched you sleep through Saturdays and stumble through Sundays.

And now, he just watches.

You drop your gaze first.
Because you can't hold his.
Because shame has a weight, and today, it looks like a kid's eyes staring right through you.

He doesn't speak.

And somehow, that silence hits harder than any lecture.

Because in that moment, the most honest thing in the room…
is his disappointment.

Dinner Left Untouched

The plate's still there.
Full. Cold. Untouched.

Mac and cheese, from the box — the kind he usually inhales.
Steamless now. Fork sitting beside it like it gave up, too.

You made it during one of those moments you thought might count.
When you still believed that *showing up* could fix things.
When you told yourself, *"At least I tried."*

But he didn't eat.
Didn't even sit.

Just looked at it… then at you… and walked to his room.
Quiet. No drama. No tears. Just absence.

And that emptiness at the table?
It screams louder than anything he could've said.

You sit down in the chair across from the untouched plate.
Lean forward like you're praying.
Stare at the congealed cheese like it holds an answer.

Your stomach twists.

Not from hunger.
From the ache of being invisible to someone who used to think you were everything.

You whisper, "I'm sorry," but he's not there to hear it.
Maybe he wouldn't believe it anyway.

And that single plate,
cooling in silence,
becomes the most honest reflection of where things stand.

This isn't about dinner.
This is about how many times love has knocked…
and found no one home.

Dinner Left Untouched

You sit at the kitchen table without really sitting.

It's more like folding into the chair. Like gravity finally won.

There's a plate in front of you. Something you microwaved. You think.
It's hard to remember what exactly. Frozen lasagna, maybe?
Still warm. But cooling.

You haven't touched it.
Your fork's in your hand. But your hand isn't moving.

You're staring through the food like it might disappear if you wait long enough.
Not because you're not hungry — but because hunger doesn't matter when your stomach's full of shame.

The clock ticks. Somewhere a faucet drips.
Everything feels too loud for how quiet it is.

And across the table… there's another plate. Smaller.
Also untouched.

You don't even know when you set it down.
Reflex, maybe. Some echo of being a parent, or pretending to be one.
You don't remember if he said he was hungry.
You just know he's not here.

And that plate —
the untouched food, the absence, the silence —
it screams louder than anything else today.

You push your own plate away.
It scrapes across the table with a sound that feels like failure.

Then you bury your face in your hands.

Because nothing feels more like defeat

than making dinner for someone who doesn't trust you enough to sit at the table.

"You Promised Again"

You hear the words before you see him.
Quiet. Flat. No emotion.

Just a fact, dropped into the room like a pin on a map.

You look up.
He's standing by the doorway, arms crossed, backpack still on.

You don't even know how long he's been there.
Maybe minutes. Maybe longer.

Your mouth opens. A breath comes out. But it's not an answer.

He steps forward. One, maybe two steps closer.
Still not angry. Still not crying.
Just that same small voice with too-big eyes.

"You said it last time. And the time before that."

You try to speak. To explain.
But what would you even say?
That you didn't mean to? That you were tired? That it got away from you again?

None of that matters.

Because he's not asking a question.
He's stating a pattern.

"I believed you," he says.
And that's the one that cuts.

Because you remember it —

his face that night on the couch,
when you said you'd be better,
when you said this time was different,
when he nodded and hugged you and said, "Okay."

You broke that version of him.

And now this one?
This one's got armor.
Thin, child-sized armor built from every time he had to clean up your silence.

You take a step forward.

He doesn't move. Doesn't flinch.
Just says one more thing:

"I stopped waiting."

And then… he walks past you.
Into his room.
Door soft behind him.

No slams.
No shouts.

Just distance.

And somehow, that silence hurts more
than any "I hate you" ever could.

A Number Scribbled on a Napkin

It's still on the table.

Right where you left it.

A napkin. Folded once. Sloppy, soft edges curled at the corners like it's been sitting there for years — even though it's only been a day. Maybe two.

The ink's smudged. Blue. Written fast.
Just a name.
And a number.

You don't remember asking for it.
But you remember the hand that gave it.

It was after the meeting.
You didn't speak — just sat in the back, arms crossed like a shield.
But he saw you.
That older guy with the denim jacket and coffee breath. The one who didn't say much either.
On his way out, he tapped your shoulder. Didn't smile. Didn't preach. Just handed you the napkin like it was a quiet dare.

"If you ever want to not do this alone."

That's all he said.

And you kept it.

Not because you believed him.
But because some small, nearly dead part of you wanted to.

Now it's here.
Staring at you from the edge of the table.
Mocking you, maybe.
Inviting you, probably.
Daring you, definitely.

You pick it up.
Hold it like a lit match.

It would be so easy to tear it.
To toss it.
To pretend it was never yours.

But your hand won't let go.

You stare at the number.

And for the first time today, the thought sneaks in:

"What if I actually called?"

Not someday.
Not after the next relapse.
Not after the next apology.
Now.

Your thumb inches toward your phone.

But stops.

Because calling means **admitting**.
Calling means stepping out of the fog and saying:

"I'm not okay."
"I can't fix this alone."
"I don't want to die like this."

And that's the scariest thing in the world, isn't it?

Not drinking.
Not losing people.
Not waking up on floors or missing birthdays or jobs.

No — the scariest thing is **hope**.

Because if you call…
If you reach out…
Then it might actually have to change.

And change?

Change is terrifying.

You place the napkin back on the table.
Delicately.
Like it's sacred.

But this time — you don't look away.
You leave it there.
Still folded.
Still waiting.

And maybe, just maybe…
so are you.

PART II
THE WAR INSIDE

DAY ONE, AGAIN

Sweating Through the Morning

You wake up before your alarm.
Not because you're rested. Because your body won't let you sleep anymore.

There's no hangover.
Not because you didn't drink — but because your body's already adapted.
What you feel now is withdrawal. The ghost of what you didn't take.

Your shirt is soaked. The sheets are damp.
You feel like you slept in a storm that only you could see.
And maybe you did.

Your hands tremble slightly as you sit up.
That faint buzz under the skin.
Not panic. Not hunger.
It's the ache of absence.

You drag yourself to the bathroom.
Not to clean up.
Just to check: Are you still in there?

You look in the mirror. Again.

The same face. But this time, the eyes are different.

They're not angry.
They're not empty.

They're waiting.

Waiting to see if today…
you'll choose something else.

You stand under the shower too long. The water's not cold, not hot — just there.
It runs over your skin like it's trying to rinse off everything you can't name.

Somewhere around your third exhale, you whisper the truth —
to no one but the water:

"God, I don't want to do this again."

But you already are.

The Circle of Strangers

You don't know why you came.
Maybe it was guilt. Maybe fear.
Or maybe that voicemail — the one you didn't answer — dug just deep enough to move your legs.

The building is old. Church basement or something like it. Plastic chairs in a half-circle. Fluorescent lights. That smell — faint coffee, cleaning supplies, something human underneath.

You walk in like a shadow. Quiet. Avoiding eye contact. Jacket zipped too high, hands shoved too deep into your pockets. Like if you stay small enough, no one will notice you don't belong.

But they do.

They always do.

Still… no one says it.

Someone nods. A woman in her fifties with eyes that look like they've seen the worst and are still standing. A guy with a beard gives you a seat with a half-smile that doesn't reach his eyes. You sit. Not because you feel safe, but because leaving would take more courage than you've got right now.

There's a rhythm here. Not spoken, but felt. People pass a piece of paper around — names. You don't take the pen. You just shake your head once, barely. They get it. No pressure.

Someone starts talking. You don't catch the beginning. Just pieces.

"…two years last week. Didn't think I'd make it past two days…"

"…my kid finally looked me in the eyes again…"

"…still dream about it sometimes — waking up with that taste in my mouth…"

It's like sitting in a room with versions of yourself you haven't met yet. Past, future, sideways.

One guy says he's grateful.
Grateful.

You almost scoff. But you don't.
Because something in you — the part that's still not completely numb —
wants to understand what that word even means anymore.

You stare at the floor.
You count your breaths.
You sit still.
And for now, that's enough.

Because you showed up.

And today… that's the only victory you've got.

Sitting but Not Staying

You're still there.

Same folding chair. Same peeling linoleum floor. Same coffee machine wheezing in the corner like it's tired too.

The group shifts. Someone new shares. Someone old nods. Someone else scratches their arm like they're itching for more than answers.

You hear words — sentences strung like survival ropes:

"…every morning I still smell it in my dreams."

"…I lied to everyone. Including myself."

"…the worst part wasn't losing my family. It was knowing I deserved it."

You sit. Still. Silent.

But inside?

You're pacing. Screaming. Bargaining.

You didn't sign anything. You didn't raise your hand. You haven't said your name.

You're not ready to say, "I'm Mike. And I'm—"

No.

Not yet.

Because saying it makes it real.

And you're not sure you're ready for reality.

So you sit.

Not like someone who belongs. Like someone who's casing the place. Like someone preparing their exit before the second round of coffee is poured.

You catch someone's eyes — briefly. He gives a nod. The kind that says, "I was you, too."

You look away.

You don't want to be seen. But part of you does.

And maybe that's why you haven't left yet.

You're sitting, yes.

But you haven't decided to stay.

Not really.

Not yet.

The Coffee Tastes Like Guilt

You pour a cup during the break. Not because you want coffee — you don't even like how it tastes anymore. But because holding something gives your hands a job. Because sipping gives you an excuse not to talk.

It's instant. Bitter. Thin. Too hot. Too familiar.

You take a sip anyway.

And it tastes like every excuse you ever made.

Like the morning after a promise.

Like the aftertaste of "I swear this was the last time."

You stand near the wall. Not quite in the circle, not quite outside it. Just far enough to pretend you're just "passing through."

Someone cracks a joke about sugar packets being the new addiction.

The room chuckles. You don't.

Because you remember real addiction — the kind that makes you lie to people you love while looking them dead in the eye.

You stare into the cup like it might tell you what to do.

All it does is steam.

And in that moment, you realize something:

You're not just drinking coffee.

You're swallowing shame.

One bitter mouthful at a time.

THE HOUR
THAT NEVER ENDS

Tremors and Regret

The second half of the meeting starts, but time doesn't.

At least, it doesn't feel like it.

You sit back in your chair. Arms crossed. Eyes forward. But your mind is sprinting through memories like they're flashing warning signs. Every story someone shares feels like a mirror — cracked, warped, but still reflecting something you recognize.

Someone says, "It's not the drinking. It's the thinking."

And damn if that doesn't land harder than it should.

Because you haven't had a drink today. But your thoughts? They're still drunk. Still stumbling over guilt, bumping into grief, knocking over hope like it's made of glass.

You look at the clock.

It's been nine minutes.

Nine.

You swear it's been an hour. Maybe two. Maybe a year.

A man across the room talks about losing his family. A woman says she walked out of her own birthday party because the cake reminded her of the person she used to be. Someone else says they relapsed in a hotel bathroom while their mom was dying.

No one gasps. No one judges.

They just nod. Like pain is a language they all speak fluently.

You shift in your seat.

The plastic groans under your weight.

Your body wants to run.

Your mind wants to hide.

But your feet stay still.

Because something in you — the smallest, quietest part — doesn't want to start over tomorrow.

Not again.

Not from zero.

So you stay.

Even though it feels like forever.

Because maybe staying…

just this once…

is the beginning of something that finally ends.

The Bottle on the Shelf

You're home.

Not because you wanted to be. But because it's the only place left to go.

The air inside your apartment feels stale, like everything's holding its breath — waiting to see what version of you walked in this time.

You drop your keys on the counter. They clatter louder than they should. You leave your jacket on the floor. Your shoes too. You don't care.

You head straight for the kitchen.

The lights are off, but you know exactly where it is.

Top shelf. Back corner. Behind the old cereal box and the unopened can of lentil soup you're never going to eat.

You open the cupboard.

And there it is.

Still full. Still waiting. Like it never left.

A bottle.

Not fancy. Not expensive. Just familiar. The kind that doesn't need a label anymore because the shape alone knows your grip.

You stare at it like it spoke your name.

And maybe it did — not out loud, but in that way ghosts whisper in old houses.

You reach for it.

Not fast. Not impulsive. Slow. Like ritual. Like habit. Like muscle memory soaked in pain.

Your fingers graze the neck.

But then they stop.

You don't pull it down.

You just hold the edge of the shelf. Like you're steadying yourself against something much heavier than wood.

And you ask:

"Why is this still here?"

You know the answer.

Because part of you wanted the option.

Because throwing it away felt too final.

Because keeping it meant maybe you hadn't really given up yet.

You stare for a long time.

The bottle doesn't move. Doesn't judge. Just sits there — patient. Eternal. Like a god you used to worship and still sometimes miss.

And that's what hurts the most.

Not the temptation.

The familiarity.

You close the cabinet slowly.

Not because you've won.

But because — for tonight — you haven't lost.

Breathing in Minutes

You step back from the shelf like it almost pulled you in.

Your chest tightens — not in panic, but in pressure. Like your ribs are trying to hold in something heavy and invisible.

You lean on the counter. Both hands flat. Palms sweating.

The bottle is still there. Unmoved. Unopened.

You didn't win.
But you didn't lose either.

So now, you breathe.

Not in hours. Not in days.

In minutes.

One at a time.

The way people do in emergency rooms. Or after car crashes. Or at funerals.

You try to focus on something simple.

The hum of the refrigerator. The grain of the cabinet wood. The faint smell of old toast.

Something real. Something now.

Because if you drift even a few inches into memory, you'll start justifying again. Bargaining. Rationalizing.

"If I just take one…"

"If I just hold it…"

"If I pour it out, then maybe I deserve another."

But you don't move.

You stay still.

Like a soldier in a minefield who just heard the click under his boot.

One wrong shift — and it's over.

So instead, you stand there. Not strong. Not brave.

Just… breathing.

In minutes.

Because that's what this is now:

Recovery.

Not a sunrise.

Not a breakthrough.

Just the slow decision to stay upright.

One goddamn minute at a time.

One Small Victory, One Shaky Breath

You don't call it a win.
Not out loud. Not even in your own head.

You just breathe.

You're still in the kitchen. Still barefoot. Still shaky. But the bottle stayed on the shelf.

That matters.
Even if no one saw it.
Even if no one cheers.

You open a cabinet. Grab instant coffee. The cheapest kind — bitter and brown and honest. You boil water. One movement at a time, like each step is part of something sacred.

Because today, it is.

The cup is chipped. The spoon clinks. You stir too long. Not because it needs it — but because you do.

You need a rhythm. A sound. A purpose, even if it's just dissolving powder in hot water.

You sit at the table.
You drink it slowly.

And with each sip, something begins to steady in you.
Not everything. Not the guilt. Not the shame.
But your breath.
Your hands.

It's not strength. Not yet.
But it's not collapse either.

You whisper — not for anyone else, just for you:

"I didn't drink."

That's it.

No speech. No plan. No promises.

Just a line in the sand —
drawn with a trembling hand,
but drawn all the same.

And for the first time in too long,

you don't feel proud.
But you don't feel hopeless either.

You feel… present.

Still broken. Still scared.
But present.

And maybe — just maybe — that's how rebuilding begins.

Not with triumph.

But with one small victory…
and one shaky breath.

THE SUPERMARKET GHOSTS

Aisle 7 Is a Minefield

You think you're ready to face the world.
You're not.

You tell yourself it's just groceries.
Just eggs. Bread. Something frozen.
Like the act of pushing a cart can somehow make you feel normal again.

But the moment those sliding glass doors part with a hiss,
you feel it.

The artificial light, too bright. The music, too happy.
The people, too alive.

You grip the handle of the cart like it's a lifeline.
And you move cautious — not because you're browsing,
but because you're scanning for exits.

Aisle 7 hits hardest.

You don't even need anything there. But your body turns anyway.
You know why.

That's where you used to buy it.
That brand. That shape. That color of the label.

And there it is — on the shelf.

Unbothered. Innocent. Waiting.

Like it hasn't ruined anything.

You stare at it too long.
Long enough for a stranger to pass you and glance.
Just a second too long. But enough.

And that's when the memory hits.

Her hand on yours, once.
The way she laughed when you reached for the cheap stuff.
The way you laughed too — before the laughing stopped.

You blink hard.
Turn away.
Grab a box of cereal you don't even like.

Because if you stand there any longer,
you might not move at all.

And you already know what happens when you don't move.

Flashbacks in the Freezer Section

You didn't come here for much. Just a few things. Bread. Milk.
Something microwavable.
But now you're frozen.
Literally.

Standing in front of the freezer doors, staring at a row of pizzas you'll never eat.

The cold fogs the glass.
And something in you fogs too.

Because right here—right in this spot—
you remember.

It was six months ago.
Before everything cracked open.

He was with you.
Your son.
Wearing that ridiculous dinosaur hoodie.
Asking if you could get waffles instead of toast.
You laughed.
Actually laughed.
And said yes.

And she was there too.
Behind the cart.
Looking at you like she still believed you could come back.

It wasn't perfect.
But it was something.
It was **almost** a family.

And now?

You're standing in the same spot.
No cart.
No kid.
No her.

Just a man pretending to choose between frozen brands while trying not to break apart in public.

The fan in the freezer hums.
The glass vibrates under your fingertips.
And your reflection—ghosted by the frost—stares back like it's asking what the hell happened to that moment.
To that man.

You blink.

Shake it off.
Open the door like it's just shopping.
Grab something random.
Anything.

You keep walking.

But part of you stayed behind—
on that tiled floor,
by the frozen waffles,
remembering how it used to feel
to be wanted.

The Smile That Wasn't Meant for Him

You're still pushing the cart.

Still pretending.

You pass the bakery section — glazed things, golden things, things that look like they were made for better mornings than yours.

And then you see her.

Not *her* her.

Just… someone.

A woman with a toddler in her cart. He's messing with a juice box, and she's laughing — that full-bodied kind of laugh that makes her tilt her head back a little, like joy surprised her.

And for half a second, she looks up.

At you.

And smiles.

Not a flirt. Not even polite.

Just reflex. The way people do when they see another human and want the world to stay kind.

But your body catches it wrong.

Like you were starving and someone waved food from a locked window.

Because that smile?

It wasn't for you.

Not really.

It was for the *idea* of you — the clean, calm man she thought she saw.

Not the wreck holding a box of frozen something and barely breathing.

You nod, because what else can you do?

And you walk on.

But it lingers.

That second of warmth.

That second of human.

And how fast it vanished once she looked away.

Escape With Eggs and Shame

You don't remember what you grabbed.

Eggs, maybe. Some bread. A bottle of something non-alcoholic that still makes your hands shake when you hold it.

You're not shopping anymore. You're escaping.

Your feet move, but your head's still in Aisle 7. Still in the freezer fog. Still watching the version of yourself that had something to lose.

You move to the self-checkout, because human eyes feel too sharp right now. You scan items like you're defusing a bomb.

Beep. Bread.

Beep. Eggs.

Beep. Guilt.

The machine asks if you have a loyalty card.

You almost laugh.

Loyalty?

You've been loyal to all the wrong things for years.

You pay. Bag your shame in plastic. Avoid the eyes of the teenage cashier restocking gum.

And then you're outside.

The air hits different.

Not fresh — just wide. Too wide.

You walk fast. Maybe too fast. Like if you stop, the memory will catch up.

And then you're in your car.

Not safe. Just… hidden.

You sit with the bag on your lap like it might spill your secrets.

The steering wheel is cold. Your fingers press into it harder than they need to.

You take one breath.

Then another.

Then one more.

The car is silent.

Except for the eggs shifting in the bag — the sound of something whole that hasn't broken yet.

You stare through the windshield at nothing in particular.

And you realize:

You didn't buy dinner. You didn't buy enough.

But somehow, it still cost you everything.

THE FUCK-IT NIGHT

Darkness That Feels Like Home

It starts around 8:17 PM.

You're back in your apartment. Bag on the counter. Groceries unpacked, sort of. Waffles in the freezer. Eggs in the fridge. One of them cracked. Fitting.

The lights are on, but dim. You didn't bother fixing the bulb in the hallway again. The shadows stretch longer here. Like they've been waiting for you.

The TV murmurs in the background — some show you've seen a hundred times but can't name. It's just noise now. White noise for a brain that can't sit still.

And that's when it happens.

The shift.

That slow, familiar slide from discomfort into surrender. It doesn't scream. It sighs. Quiet. Heavy. Inevitable.

Your body moves without asking. You're not pacing, not storming — just… drifting. Like a boat with its anchor cut loose.

You sit on the floor. Back against the couch. Legs stretched, head tipped back, eyes on the ceiling like it might blink first.

There's no bottle in your hand. Not yet. But your fingers curl like they miss it.

You think:
"Why not?"
"It's been a shit day."
"I stayed sober. I did the thing."

And underneath all of that:
"I'm tired."

Not sleepy. Not physically worn out.
Tired like your soul's been scraping against asphalt for miles.

The kind of tired where numb feels like comfort.
Where silence feels like arms.
Where darkness doesn't scare you — it feels like home.

You close your eyes.

And you say it.
Out loud this time.
The three words that always show up before relapse:

"Fuck it. Whatever."

But something stops you.

Not strength.

Not resolve.

Just a breath.
One inhale that stutters.
One moment that cracks through the numb.

You stay on the floor.
Not moving.

Not drinking.
Just… holding.

Holding the darkness without letting it climb in.

And for tonight, maybe that's enough.

"What's the Point?"

You don't even remember walking home.

The streetlights blur. The sidewalk shifts. It's like the world lost its outline and you're moving through the sketch of it. A version of the night that gave up trying to look real.

You fumble for your keys. Drop them. Twice. The lock finally clicks. The door creaks open.

Inside: silence.

Not peaceful. Not quiet.

Just that hollow sort of silence that makes you wonder if the walls even bother listening anymore.

You kick off your shoes. Or maybe you don't. You're not sure. One lands near the couch, the other — wherever.

You stand in the middle of the room.

Not moving. Not thinking.

Just… suspended.

"What's the point?"

You don't say it out loud, but it's there. Thick in the air. Floating between your ribs.

What's the point of staying sober?

What's the point of going back to meetings?

What's the point of pretending this story turns out different?

You sit on the couch like it's the last chair in the world.

Not because you're tired — you passed tired two days ago — but because there's nowhere else to go.

You stare at nothing.

And nothing stares back.

Your hands twitch. Your knee bounces. Your breath catches.

The bottle's still in the cabinet. You know that.

It's not calling to you.

Not really.

It doesn't need to.

It just waits.

Like it always does.

You close your eyes and see yourself reaching for it. You feel the relief before it happens. The warmth. The numb. The vanish.

You open your eyes.

Still there.

Still choosing.

Still not doing it.

But God, it's close tonight.

So close it hums in your bones.

One Message That Lands

You don't hear the buzz.
You feel it.
That little vibration on the table like a second heartbeat.

You think about ignoring it.
You think about smashing your phone.
You think about never hearing from anyone again.

But something in you moves.
Fingers slow. Breath slower.

The screen lights up.

Chris.
Again.

No guilt. No long paragraph.
Just three words:

"Still here, brother."

That's it.

No demands. No questions.
No pressure to reply.

Just presence.

And somehow, that breaks something.

Not in a dramatic way.
No tears.
No cinematic music cue.
Just a crack — in the wall you've been building brick by quiet brick.

Because that one message?

It doesn't fix anything.
But it reminds you of something you'd almost forgotten:

You are *not* invisible.

And not everyone has walked away.

You stare at the words for a long time.
Thumb hovering. Chest tight.

You don't reply. Not yet.

But you don't delete it either.

And that's something.

A Choice Made Barefoot

You're not sure how long you've been sitting.

Could be minutes. Could be hours. Time's a blur when your body's still but your thoughts won't stop pacing.

Your feet are bare. You notice that now.

Cold against the tile.

You stand. Slowly. Like your limbs don't quite trust you yet.

The house feels like it's holding its breath.

And you walk.

Not with purpose. Not with some grand intention.

Just forward. Barefoot.

Past the sink with its crusted dishes. Past the jacket you should've hung up three days ago. Past the drawer that still has her handwriting on a Post-it note inside.

You stop in front of the cabinet.

That cabinet.

The one that always had what you needed.
The one that whispered comfort when the world went silent.
The one that still holds a bottle — not calling, not screaming — just waiting.

Your hand hovers near the handle.

You feel the pulse in your fingertips.
You could open it. You could.
No one would know.

Except you.

You drop your hand.

Turn away.

Not in triumph.

In defiance.

A small one.
A quiet one.

But still… a choice.

And you made it barefoot.
Without armor. Without noise.
Without even hope.

Just a man, alone in a kitchen, choosing to stay upright for one more breath.

And sometimes, that's the whole war.

THE PHOTO ON THE FRIDGE

Dust on Old Dreams

The kitchen light buzzes overhead — that tired hum of a bulb that's been holding on too long.
You stand in front of the fridge, hand still on the handle, but you're not opening it.

Not yet.

Because your eyes land on something else.

A photo.

Crooked. Faded. Edges curling.
Pinned beneath a magnet shaped like a palm tree —
from that beach trip.
The one you **do** remember.

You can still feel the sand between your toes.
His tiny fingers in your hand.
His laughter bursting as he ran from the waves, yelling, "Too cold!"
The way she looked at you —
book in her lap, legs stretched out, eyes soft.
Like she still believed you could come back to yourself.

It's you. And him.
Your son on your shoulders, maybe four years old.

His hair's wild from the wind.
You're both laughing — mouths wide open, eyes squinting like the sun was too much but the joy was more.

You don't remember the exact moment.
But you remember the feeling.

Back when smiles came easy.
Back when weekends weren't warnings.

You lean in.
Brush off the light layer of dust that settled across his face.
And yours.
Almost like time itself was trying to forget you.

The magnet slips. The photo tilts.

You catch it — gently. As if it were glass.
As if one wrong move could crack the past wide open.

You hold it in your hand now.
And something twists in your chest.

Not regret.
Not nostalgia.
Something quieter. Sadder.

Like hope… gone stale.

Because this picture — this captured second —
it's a version of you that believed.

A man who thought he could be the dad he never had.
The partner who didn't disappear.
The one who showed up. Stayed.

You trace your thumb over the faces.
Like contact could reverse time.

It can't.

The kitchen stays quiet.
The fridge hums on.

And you place the photo back — not where it was —
but straighter now.

You don't know why.

Maybe it's nothing.
Or maybe…
maybe it's the first thing you've tried to fix in a long time.

That Grin, That Hope

You find it by accident.

Tucked in a drawer you haven't opened in months. Maybe longer.

You were looking for batteries. Or tape. Or a charger that no longer fits anything.

But instead —
you find a photo strip.

The kind from a booth. Black and white. Grainy.

And there he is.

Your son. Maybe five this time. His head tilted toward you in the first frame, eyebrows raised in mock surprise. In the second — a full belly laugh, nose scrunched, pure mischief.
In the third — your face next to his, both of you grinning like the world had just told you a beautiful secret.

And the last one?

That one's quieter.

You're not smiling as wide. He is.
But you're looking at him — not the camera.
Like you're trying to memorize something you know you'll need later.

You sit down on the floor.

Right there. Drawer still open. The world on pause.

And you stare at that grin.

His.

Yours.

The kind of grin that doesn't come from being entertained — but from being whole, even just for a second.

It's not just joy in those photos.

It's hope.

Hope you didn't even know you had that day.

Hope that maybe you could do this.

Hope that maybe love could be enough.

And now, in this dim room, holding a memory in your hand, you wonder:

Is it still in you?

That version of you?

The one who laughed without effort.
The one who looked at his kid like he was the center of the galaxy.

You press the photo strip to your chest.

Close your eyes.

And for the first time in a long time,

you don't feel lost.
Just… paused.
Like maybe something inside is waiting.
Still holding on.
Still believing, even if it's quiet.

Still carrying that grin.
Still reaching for that hope.

He Was Real Once

You sit down at the kitchen table, the photo still fresh in your mind —

not just the image, but the weight of it.
The truth it held up like a mirror.

There was a version of you that existed.
Not perfect. Not fixed.
But *real*.

You remember his laugh — not just your son's, but yours.
That cracked, unfiltered kind. The kind you didn't have to earn.
It came easy then.
Before everything got buried under lies and half-restarts and long nights.

You weren't always this ghost in your own house.

You weren't always hollow behind the eyes.

There was a man who showed up early.
Who held doors open.
Who remembered birthdays and meant it when he said, "I'll be home soon."

You don't know when exactly he disappeared.
But you remember the trail he left behind.

The way your kid used to run toward the door when you came home.
The way she used to rest her head on your shoulder, not out of habit, but trust.
The way you used to look at your own reflection and not flinch.

He was real.

That man.

Not a fantasy. Not a dream.
He lived.
He walked.
He laughed with his whole chest.

And maybe that's the worst part.
Because if he was real once…

Then what the hell happened?

What *happened* to you?

The chair creaks beneath you as you shift.
The silence in the room grows teeth again.
But you don't get up.

Because maybe, if he was real once…

He can be real again.

Maybe that's not naive.
Maybe it's the first honest thought you've had all day.

Maybe He Still Is

You stand in front of the bathroom mirror again —
the place where this whole spiral feels like it always begins.

But this time, you're not avoiding your reflection.
You're staring straight into it.

And it hits you:

You still flinch, but not as much.

Your eyes are tired, yes —
but they're watching now.
Not just looking through things, but *at* them.
At you.

There's a pulse in your neck.
A breath that actually makes it to your lungs.

And maybe that's the difference.

You run a hand over your jaw. The stubble is rough.
There's a tiny nick near your lip.
Your skin is a battlefield — but it's still *yours*.

You lean in.

Closer than you've let yourself in a long time.

And there —
between the wreckage,
beneath the years of damage,
behind the shame and silence —
you catch something.

Faint. Flickering.
Like a pilot light that refused to go out.

He's still in there.
That man you were.
That man you miss.

Not gone.
Just… buried.
Under bottles and bruises and broken promises.
But not dead.

Not erased.

Not irredeemable.

You press your palm flat against the mirror.
And whisper — not with your mouth, but with your heart:

"I still see you."

And for a second — just one clean second —
you believe it.

Not as a fantasy.
Not as a hope.

But as a fact.

He may be hidden.
But he's still here.

And maybe…
maybe he's waiting on *you*
to come back.

THE FIRST TIME HE SPOKE

Sweaty Palms, Dry Throat

The chair beneath you feels like punishment. Too hard. Too loud when it creaks under your weight.
Your hands are clammy. Knees bouncing. Eyes fixed on the coffee stain near your shoe like it might swallow you whole if you stare long enough.

Someone's sharing. Their voice is steady. Almost too steady.
You're not listening, not really.
You're **counting your breaths**, like each one is buying you more time not to speak.

But then there's a pause.

A silence that stretches just long enough to make the whole room turn.

And before your brain can catch your mouth—

You say it.

"I'm Mike."

Your voice cracks on the name.

It sounds too sharp in the air.
Too *real*.

You don't even say the whole thing.
Not the part about drinking. Not the part about losing everything.
Just the name.

But it's enough.

Because it's the **first time in a long time you've claimed your own skin**.

Your palms sweat harder now. Your throat tightens like it's trying to pull the words back.

But they're out there.

Floating. Landing.

And nobody laughs.

Nobody winces.

Someone nods.

That's it.

Not a standing ovation.
Just a nod.

But somehow, that tiny gesture feels louder than applause.

Because in this room, silence isn't **emptiness**.

It's **witnessing**.

And for the first time…
you realize you're not invisible.

You're not gone.

You're just beginning to come back.
One breath, one sentence at a time.

Words That Spill, Then Snap

You don't plan what you're going to say.

There's no speech. No script. No rehearsed lines running laps in your head.

Just heat in your palms. Tightness in your chest. And that faint shake in your jaw like it's holding something too heavy for too long.

You clear your throat. Once. Twice.

And then it happens.

Words — stumbling over each other, like they've been trapped too long behind your teeth and now they're fighting to get out.

"I don't know where it went wrong. I mean, I do… but I don't. One day I was holding my son on the beach, and the next I was lying about where I'd been."

It's messy. Disjointed. Honest.

"They say it's a disease. But sometimes it just feels like I made a thousand tiny wrong choices that added up to… this."

Your voice cracks.

Someone shifts in their chair.

You hear yourself say more than you meant to:

"I used to laugh. Like, really laugh. And now I wake up hoping I don't feel anything at all."

And then — silence.

Because the next word catches in your throat. Snaps like a string pulled too tight.

You close your mouth.

The air feels thick. Heavy with everything you just said. And everything you couldn't.

No one claps. No one gasps.

But someone nods. Another clears their throat.

And someone across the room says, "Yeah."

Just that.

"Yeah."

And somehow, it's enough.

The Room Holds Its Breath

You step back.
Not with your feet—inside.
The words feel too far out.

Your jaw tightens; shoulders brace.
You wait for impact.
Judgment. Pity. The flinch.

It doesn't come.

No laughs. No phone glow.
The vent hums; chairs don't scrape.
The room stays with you.

A man across the circle nods.
Once. Small. Steady.

It finds your spine like a palm:
I know.

You feel it more than see it.
Heat in the ribs loosens.
Breath drops lower.

Someone heard you—and didn't look away.

No speeches. No fixes. No rescue.
Just presence.

In that quiet you notice this:
you're still here,
not crazy,
not invisible,
not alone.

Seen—enough to lift your eyes..

Someone Nods. That's Enough.

You step back.

Not physically. Just… inside. Like you said too much. Like the words that just left your mouth weren't meant to be spoken out loud, especially not here. Especially not to them.

You wait for something.

Judgment. Pity. Awkward silence.

Anything.

But no one laughs. No one shifts away. No one checks their phone like they're trying to escape what you just said.

Instead, someone nods.

Just once.

A man across the circle. Hoodie. Tired eyes. Maybe fifty, maybe thirty—it's hard to tell with some kinds of living.

The nod isn't big. It's not dramatic. Just a small, solid motion.

But it lands.

It lands like a hand on your back that says:
"I know."

You feel it more than you see it.

And it does something strange to the tightness in your chest. Loosens it. Just a little.

Because someone heard you.
Someone let it in.
And instead of turning away—they nodded.

That's it.

No speech.
No hug.
No answers.

Just presence.

And right now, that's enough.

More than enough.

Because it means:

You're not the only one.
You're not crazy.
You're not invisible.

You're here.

And someone sees you.

THE CLOSED DOOR

Reaching Out

You sit alone in the hallway after the meeting.

The others have shuffled out—some with polite goodbyes, some with quiet urgency, like staying too long might reopen wounds they've only just stitched.

But you linger.

The air's still warm from the group. Still thick with things that weren't said out loud but were felt.

You take out your phone.

Your thumb hovers over Chris's name again.

No new messages. No missed calls.

But tonight, you don't need a new message.

You need to send one.

You open the thread. That old one, still sitting there with his last words:

"Still here, brother."

You breathe in.

Out.

And type:

"I spoke tonight. First time."

You stare at it.

Backspace once.

Then retype it.

"I spoke tonight. Finally."

You hit send before you can talk yourself out of it.

It goes. Blue bubble. Delivered.

No fanfare. No instant reply.

Just the quiet satisfaction of doing something that scares you.

Not because you expect a rescue.

Not because it'll fix anything.

But because *reaching out* is how things *start* to shift.

Because connection doesn't always come crashing in.

Sometimes, it knocks.

Soft.

And sometimes…

you have to open the door first.

The Voice That Doesn't Answer

You call.

Not in a rush. Not in a panic.

Just… quietly.

Phone pressed to your ear, breath held like it might tip the scales.

It rings.

Once.

Twice.

Three times.

You already know how this ends.

But you still wait.

Because maybe — just maybe — this time it won't go to voicemail.

It does.

Chris's voice again. Calm. Even. Kind.

"Hey, it's Chris. You know what to do."

Beep.

You freeze.

Your mouth opens, but your voice doesn't come.

You want to say:
"Thanks."
"I'm still here."
"I almost drank tonight."

But what comes out instead is… nothing.

Just the soft sound of your breath.
And then: click.

You end the call.

And stand there — phone still in your hand, shame climbing up your spine like cold water.

It wasn't a rejection. It wasn't a goodbye.

But it felt like a door stayed closed.

And maybe the hardest part?

You're not mad.

Because deep down, you get it.

People have lives. People sleep. People miss calls.

But the voice that didn't answer?

It wasn't his.

It was yours.

The one inside you that still doesn't know how to ask for help when it matters most.
That still chokes on honesty.
That still hasn't forgiven itself enough to believe it deserves a reply.

You put the phone down.

And the silence after the call isn't empty.

It's heavy.

But somehow —
you're still standing in it.

No Doesn't Mean Never

You stare at the phone like it betrayed you.

But it didn't.

It just did what phones do — rang, waited, fell silent.

The word "no" never came.
But your mind fills it in anyway.

Because silence feels like rejection when you're already on the edge.

You walk to the window.
Barefoot again.
The tile cold, grounding.
The outside world is still there — cars, lights, someone walking their dog like it's just another night.

And maybe for them, it is.

But for you?

This was supposed to be a turning point.

And now it just feels like another quiet wall.

But then something shifts.

Not loud. Not sudden.

Just a thought that slips in like a breeze under the door:

Maybe "no" isn't forever.

Maybe "not now" doesn't mean "never."

You remember what Chris said once, the first meeting you stayed all the way through:

"If you call and I don't pick up, call again.
If I still don't pick up — keep breathing.
It just means I'm human.
And so are you."

You didn't get it then.

But maybe you do now.

Because you didn't drink.

Because you reached out.

Because tomorrow might be different.

Because "no" isn't the end.

It's just the pause before "try again."

Standing Still and Not Drinking

You're not moving.
Not pacing, not fixing anything, not calling anyone.

Just standing.

In the center of the kitchen, where the tile is still cold, where the air still smells like old decisions.

The cabinet is still there.

The bottle is still inside.

Nothing's changed.

Except you haven't opened it.

You haven't poured.

You haven't lied.

And somehow, that matters.

It doesn't feel like a win.
There's no soundtrack.
No applause.

Just stillness.

Heavy. Honest. Present.

You grip the edge of the counter like it might float away without you.

Your breath is shallow, but it's yours.
Your hands shake, but they're empty.

And you realize something:

You're standing.
Still.
And not drinking.

It doesn't sound heroic.
But it's everything.

It's a decision made in the quiet.
A boundary drawn without witnesses.
A kind of strength you can't post online.

It's boring.
It's unglamorous.
It's sober.

And tonight, that's enough.
More than enough.

Because standing still and not drinking?
That's how tomorrow gets a chance.

THE ROOM WHERE HE SLEPT ON THE FLOOR

A Couch Offered Without Words

The door opens before you knock.

Chris stands there. Same hoodie. Same silence.

But he moves aside. Just enough for you to step through.

No questions.

No looks.

Just space.

You nod — barely.
He nods back.

And then, as you step inside, he says — soft, quiet:

"I'm glad you came."

Nothing more. Nothing expected.

Inside smells like something warm was cooked hours ago but never eaten. The light is low. One lamp in the corner. A folded blanket on the couch.

You drop your bag near the wall.

It makes a soft thud.

Chris walks into the kitchen, opens a cupboard, pulls something out.

You expect a lecture. A question. Some version of *"You ready to try for real this time?"*

But instead, he comes back and places a key on the coffee table.
Doesn't say a word. Doesn't look at you.
Just places it there — like an invitation you don't have to accept.

Your throat tightens.

You don't know if it's kindness or pressure or grace.

Maybe all three.

You sit down. Slowly.
The couch creaks like it remembers you from some other night.

And for a moment, you just breathe.

You try to feel something.
Relief. Guilt. Shame. Gratitude.

But there's nothing.

Just… stillness.

And maybe that's scarier than anything.

Chris disappears into the other room. Door half-shut.
Like trust, not fully given, not fully taken.

You pull the blanket over your chest, not because you're cold — but because it feels like the only thing holding you together.

Then you hear it.

A siren in the distance.

Not close. But familiar.

Your mind flashes back — your son in the backseat, fingers in his ears, whispering, "Make it stop, Daddy."

You squeeze your eyes shut.

It passes.

You breathe again.

And then, before the silence returns completely — you whisper:

"Thanks for not asking anything."

From the other room — nothing.

But that's okay.

Because this couch?

This silence?

It held you tonight.

And that's more than most things have.

Midnight Talk That Hurts

The clock says 2:11 AM.

You're not sure if you ever actually fell asleep.

Just drifted somewhere between breath and memory, eyes closed but mind wide open.

The couch is stiff. The blanket itches. But that's not why you're awake.

It's the quiet.

Too quiet.

Then — a sound. Soft steps on hardwood. Chris.

He doesn't turn on the light. Just walks past the couch into the kitchen.

Opens the fridge. Closes it again. No sound of pouring. Just the door. Just the hum.

You hear him lean against the counter.

And then, from the dark:

"Do you miss him?"

Your throat tightens.
You don't ask who.

He knows.
You know.

You don't answer right away.
Not because you're avoiding it —
but because your heart needs time to find the words your mouth forgot how to say.

Finally:

"Every damn day."

Chris exhales. It's not relief. Not judgment.
Just shared weight.

He walks back toward the living room.
Leans in the doorway. Arms crossed.

"I remember when you brought him to the meeting once. He drew superheroes in my notebook."

You manage a laugh. Small. Broken.

"Yeah… he said you looked like the Hulk."

Chris smirks. "He wasn't wrong."

Silence again. But this time it feels earned.

Then:

"Why didn't you call?" he asks.

You stare at the ceiling. Let the words settle on your chest like bricks.

"I wanted to get better first."

He nods once. Slowly.

"But you didn't."

You shake your head.

"No."

And that hurts more than anything.

But you said it.

Out loud.

In the dark.

To someone who stayed.

Chris pushes off the doorway.
Half-turns to leave, then pauses:

"Try again. Don't wait this time."

You don't reply.

But your hand grips the edge of the blanket a little tighter.

Not for warmth.

But to feel something real.

Something still here.

Shared Pain, Shared Silence

The room isn't big.
But tonight, it feels like a cathedral —
echoes made of things no one says.

You sit on one end of the couch. Chris sits on the other.
Between you — the coffee table, the key, two mugs of something warm neither of you is drinking.

No TV. No music.
Just the hum of the fridge and the ticking of a wall clock that seems too loud for what it's measuring.

Neither of you speaks.

And somehow, that feels right.

Because pain — real pain —
doesn't always need a voice.
Sometimes it just needs someone to sit next to it
and not run away.

You don't look at each other.

But you feel it.

The weight in the air. The exhaustion. The decades of trying to hold it together when no one taught you how.

At one point, Chris shifts.
Not much. Just enough for his knee to crack.

You almost laugh.
Almost.

Instead, you wrap both hands around the mug.
Let the warmth soak in.

And for once, the silence doesn't feel empty.

It feels… equal.

You're not explaining yourself.

You're not being fixed.

You're just… here.

Two men.
Two broken cups.
Holding whatever's left.

And in some quiet, strange way —
that feels like enough.

"You're Not the Only One"

The silence stretches.

Not awkward.
Not cold.
Just… full.

You're still holding the mug. The tea's gone lukewarm. Chris is in the chair opposite you, one sock half-off, his elbow on the armrest, eyes not quite meeting yours.

And then he says it.

Not like a sermon.
Not like a confession.
Just like a fact.

"You're not the only one who's messed it all up."

You don't move.

Because those words hit harder than blame.

They don't excuse you.
They just… include you.

"I didn't stop because I got strong," he adds.
"I stopped because I got scared."

You blink. Once.

"Scared of losing my kid. Scared of waking up in a hospital. Scared of waking up and not being scared anymore."

That one lands deep.

Because you know that fear too — the kind that keeps you frozen, and the kind that finally pushes you to move.

You nod.

Not to agree.
To acknowledge.

He leans forward.

"But I didn't do it alone. I still don't."

You stare into the space between your knees.

"You're not the only one," he says again.
"But you're the only one who can decide if it ends here."

That hangs in the air.
Heavy. Unavoidable.

You don't answer.

But inside — something shifts.

Not loudly. Not clearly.
But enough to make room for breath.

And in that breath…

maybe a beginning.

PART III
WHEN NOTHING HAPPENS, BUT EVERYTHING CHANGES

THE 30TH DAY

No Parade, Just Coffee

You wake up on the 30th day.

Not to applause.
Not to clarity.
Not to a sunrise that suddenly makes sense of everything.

Just… coffee.

Same chipped mug. Same burnt smell from the cheap machine.
Same kitchen light that flickers once before staying on.

Thirty days.

A whole damn month without a drink.
And yet — the sky looks the same.
The mirror still startles you.
The ache in your chest hasn't packed its bags.

You sit at the table.
You don't scroll. Don't call. Don't post.
Just sip.

No parade.
No choir singing redemption songs.

Just the bitter taste of something ordinary.
Something steady.

And maybe that's what makes it holy.

Because this isn't about fireworks or finish lines.
It's about choosing the same small "yes" again —
when no one's clapping.
When no one's watching.
When the high of starting is long gone,
and all that's left is the hum of "keep going."

You lean back in the chair.
Look at the fridge. The photo still hangs there — straight.
You didn't touch it this morning.

But it touched you.

Because thirty days ago,
you didn't think you'd still be here.
You didn't think you'd want to be.

And now?

You're not healed.
Not whole.
But you're here.

Drinking coffee.
Not whiskey.

No parade.
Just presence.

And maybe that's the beginning
of something better than applause.

The Craving That Fades, Slowly

It doesn't disappear with fanfare.

No fireworks. No grand goodbye.
No dramatic moment where the bottle whispers its last word and vanishes.

Instead, it fades.

Slowly.

Like a song you've played too many times,
and one day realize… you don't need to hear it again.

It's still there — in flashes.
The thought when you pass the bar on 8th.
The itch when the rain hits just right.
The echo when you sit in the same chair, at the same hour, in the same silence.

But it doesn't roar anymore.

Now it sighs.
It flickers instead of flames.
It taps your shoulder, but doesn't grab your throat.

You stand in the grocery store aisle and don't turn your head when you pass the liquor section.
You sit in your car outside a meeting and don't need to talk yourself into going.
You hear laughter from the patio of a pub and don't feel like the world left you behind.

You still feel the ache sometimes —
not for the drink, but for what it promised.

Ease.
Silence.
Oblivion.

But now you know that was never real.

It was a trade.

And the cost was always higher than you could afford.

Today, you take a deep breath.
You exhale — slow, steady.
You feel the craving lean in.

And you say, almost softly:

"Not today."

Not with anger.
Not with force.
Just a choice.

And the craving?

It doesn't argue.
It just drifts back into the quiet.

Still there.
But further away than it used to be.

And that distance?
That space between impulse and action?

That's where freedom begins.

Feeling Numb but New

You wake up without panic.

No jolt. No mental checklist of who you hurt last night.
No desperate scramble to remember where your phone is, or if you texted someone something you'll regret.

Just quiet.

And it's strange.

Almost… unsettling.

Because chaos was your rhythm for so long, this stillness feels like a stranger in your bed.

You sit up.
The room's the same — same window, same dusty shelf, same cracked phone screen on the nightstand.
But it feels different. Like the walls are giving you space instead of closing in.

You move slower. Not because you're hungover.
Because you don't have to run from anything today.

You brush your teeth.
Drink water.
Notice the sky out the window isn't gray or blue — just light.

You should feel proud. Or strong. Or at least alive.

But mostly… you feel numb.

Not bad. Not broken.

Just empty in a way that isn't bleeding anymore.

Like your body's been ringing with alarms for years, and someone finally cut the wire.

You sip coffee that actually tastes like coffee.
Not like guilt. Not like bargaining.

And you realize:

This isn't joy.

This isn't a movie ending.
This isn't fireworks.

This is day thirty-something.

This is what beginning again really looks like.

Quiet.
Uneven.
Honest.

And even if you don't feel whole yet —
even if you're not sure you ever will —

you're not drowning.

Not today.

And that?

That's new.

The Quiet Win Nobody Sees

You don't tell anyone.
Not Chris. Not the group.
Not even yourself, out loud.

But you walked past the liquor store today.

Not quickly. Not with pride.
Just… walked past.

And your chest tightened.
And your hands ached.
And your mouth remembered the shape of forgetting.

But you kept walking.

No applause.
No milestone badge.
No pat on the back.

Just a second of silence where chaos usually lives.

You bought laundry detergent instead.
And stood in line behind someone arguing over coupons.
And you hated how normal it all felt.
And loved it too.

Because standing there — bored, sober, unnoticed —
was the most alive you've felt in weeks.

You don't write it down.
You don't track it on a chart.

But somewhere deep inside, a part of you whispers:

"That counted."

You remember every dramatic failure.
Every loud regret.
Every moment you unraveled like it was a performance.

But this?

This was quiet.
This was boring.
This was victory.

You get home.
Throw the detergent on top of the machine.

You almost cry.
But not because you're sad.

Because you're still here.

And today — even without anyone noticing — you won.

THE FIRST YES

A Stranger's Question

You're leaving the meeting.
Same folding chairs. Same burnt coffee.
Same nervous shuffling of feet after the closing words.

You don't expect anything.
Just the slow shuffle toward the door,
like always.

But someone taps your arm.

A guy you've never spoken to.
You've seen him — once, maybe twice.
Always sitting in the back. Hoodie up. Eyes down.

He looks young.
Too young to be here.
But pain doesn't ask for ID.

He doesn't smile.
Doesn't stammer.
He just asks:

"Does it ever get easier?"

You freeze.

You want to laugh.

Or cry.
Or run.

Because you've asked yourself that question every damn day.

And you still don't know the answer.

But something in his face —
the weight behind his voice —
makes you stay still.

And then — for the first time —
you say it.

Not loud.
Not wise.
But honest:

"Today was okay."

His eyes flicker.

You see it.
That spark.
Not hope, exactly.
But possibility.

And it hits you:

This is what *yes* looks like.

Not dramatic.
Not shiny.
Not a speech.

Just one scarred person telling another:
"I didn't fall today."

You nod once.
He nods back.

And that's it.

He walks away.
You walk out into the night.
Cool air. Quiet sky.
Same problems.
Same weight.

But something small has shifted.

Because today,
a stranger asked the question.
And you didn't lie.

You told the truth.
And for someone else,
that might be the beginning.

And for you…
it might be the continuation.

Of what?
You're still not sure.

But it started with a question.
And an answer you didn't think you had.

Yes.
Just once.
But real.

Saying What He Needed to Hear

The room is empty now.
Chairs stacked. Lights dimmed.

That smell of coffee and paper still hanging in the air like a memory that doesn't leave.

You stayed behind —
not on purpose.
You just… didn't move.

Your legs didn't ask permission.
Your hands rested in your lap.
And for once,
the silence didn't demand to be filled.

Chris walks by with the last trash bag.
Pauses.
Doesn't say anything at first.

Then, gently:

"You good?"

You nod.

But then your mouth does something strange.
It opens.

And out comes a sentence you didn't rehearse.
Didn't plan.

"I never thought I'd get this far."

He sets the trash down.

Looks at you. Really looks.
Not through you. Not past you.

"What far?" he asks.

You shrug.

"Thirty days. A full month. Breathing. Standing. Not picking up. Not disappearing."
Your voice cracks at the end.

He doesn't nod.
Doesn't pat your back.
Doesn't say, "Good job."

He says something else.

Quiet.
Sharp.
Right in the center of your chest.

"Then maybe it's time you stop saying, 'I'm trying.' And start saying, 'I'm doing it.'"

It lands hard.

Because you realize —
you've still been talking like you're on the edge.
Even as your feet have started learning how to stay.

You let that sit.
Let it burn a little.
Then you say the words.

"I'm doing it."

Not for him.
Not for applause.
Not even for yourself, really.

Just to hear it spoken.
Out loud.
In a room that once knew your silence better than your name.

"I'm doing it."

Chris picks the bag back up.
Smiles, just barely.

"Yeah," he says.
"You are."

And for the first time in a long time,
you believe it, too.

The Mirror Replies, "Well Done"

The bathroom is quiet.

Not haunted.
Not heavy.
Just... still.

You step inside like you've done a hundred times before —
but this time,
your body doesn't flinch at the light.

The mirror is there. Same cracks in the corner. Same rust at the base of the frame.
Same man in the reflection.

Only now — something's shifted.

You're not hiding from it.
You're not bracing for it.
You're just... looking.

Straight on.

The eyes looking back aren't fixed.
They're not proud, not glowing.
But they're clear.

Clear enough to say:

I see you.
I know what you've come through.
And I'm still here.

You run a hand across your face.
It's not a dramatic moment.
No music. No movie scene.
Just a hand. A face. A breath.

But then—

Something almost impossible:
The mirror doesn't accuse.
It doesn't flinch.

It offers something else.

Not a smile.
Not a tear.

But quiet acknowledgment.

Like it's saying:
You didn't run.
You didn't drink.
You didn't vanish.

You stayed.

And in that silence —
you hear it.

Not from your lips.
But from somewhere deeper.

A voice that sounds like your own.
Stronger than it used to.

"Well done."

Not loud.
Not grand.

But real.

And maybe for the first time,
you believe it.

Something Clicks Inside

It happens on the couch.

Not during a dramatic speech.
Not in the middle of a meeting.
Not with tears or trembling hands.

Just… a breath.

You're leaning forward, elbows on knees, trying to lace up your shoes.
And somewhere between loop and pull—
you freeze.

Something shifts.
Not loud. Not sharp. Just there.
A weight that was tangled in your chest… eases.

You sit up a little straighter.
Not because you're ready.
But because, for the first time in a long time, you're not collapsing inward.

You don't know what to call it.

But it feels like your mind stopped fighting itself—
for just a second.

No thoughts screaming.
No guilt replaying old scenes.
No voice whispering, "What's the point?"

Just a moment of quiet.
Not around you—**within you**.

You exhale.
Not because you're relaxed.
But because—**for the first time—you want to keep going.**

You finish tying your laces.

And then you whisper something, almost without knowing it left your lips:

"Maybe I don't need to be broken forever."

Not said like a hope.
Not asked like a question.
Just… released.

You glance around the room.
Same walls. Same air. Same creaky floorboard by the door.

But you're not the same man who walked in last night.

Something's different.

Not everything.
Not enough to dance over.
But enough to stand up.

And that?

That's a beginning.

THE TINY REPAIR

The Hinge That Stuck for Months

It squeaks.
That sharp, metal sound like something resisting being moved.

You stop in the hallway, look back toward the door.
The closet one. The one that never quite closed right.

It's been that way for months. Maybe longer.
A hinge bent just enough to catch.
A door that always needed a nudge, a shove, a little frustration.

You used to slam it.
Once with your fist.
Once with your foot.
Once — you don't even remember, but the dent is still in the drywall.

But today —
you kneel down.

No rush.
No anger.
Just… curiosity.

You open the toolbox.
Find the screwdriver.
Turn the screws slow, like you're listening to the metal.

You jiggle the hinge. It doesn't complain as much this time.

You try again.
Open. Close.
Smoother.

Not perfect.
But better.

You sit there for a second, staring at your work.
It's a door. Just a door.
But your chest feels… fuller.

Because for once —
you didn't ignore the thing that didn't work.
You didn't curse it.
You didn't blame it.
You fixed it.

And maybe —
that's how it starts.

Not with a breakthrough.
Not with applause.
But with a hinge that finally lets go.

Just enough
to close without a fight.

Screws, Sweat, and Patience

The screw won't catch.

You press harder. Angle the driver just right. Still nothing.

It's one of those tasks that looks easy. Should be easy.
But your hands sweat. Your wrist cramps.
The metal slips and you almost stab your palm.

You exhale through your nose.
Try again.

It's not just the screw.
It's everything it stands for.

Because this isn't just a loose hinge.
It's the shelf that's always been crooked.
The leg of the chair that wobbles when no one's sitting.
The drawer that sticks just enough to remind you what you haven't fixed.

You could walk away.
You've done it before.

But today?

You stay.

One turn.
Another.
Slow. Careful.

Tiny sounds of progress.
Not the kind anyone claps for.
But the kind your nervous system notices.

Because this isn't about the screw.
It's about the part of you that didn't quit after the first slip.
Or the second.

It's about choosing patience when your instinct screams rush.

It's about building something, even if it's small.
Even if no one sees it.
Even if your hands shake a little while doing it.

You tighten the last one.

Wipe your forehead with your sleeve.
Stand back.
It holds.

And something in you —
the quiet part that's been learning to trust yourself again —
it holds too.

Because sometimes, rebuilding your life
looks exactly like fixing something no one else noticed was broken.

And doing it anyway.
With screws.
With sweat.
With patience.

Finishing Something

It's not a big project.

Just a drawer that sticks when you pull it.
A shelf that's been tilted for six months.
A door that won't close unless you lift it by the handle and shove.

You've walked past it a hundred times.
Each time, telling yourself, "Later."
"Someday."
"When I'm in a better place."

But today — maybe because you're still standing,
maybe because you've started choosing stillness over escape —
you stop.

You get the screwdriver.
The old towel.
The tiny can of paint with the lid stuck on like it hasn't been touched in years.

(It hasn't.)

It's slow going.

The screw slips once.
The towel leaves lint.
You bump your elbow on the counter and curse under your breath.

But you don't leave.

You kneel down.
Get your fingers dirty.
Feel the weight of the hinge, the groove of the wood,
the quiet dignity of doing something no one will praise you for.

And you finish it.

The drawer slides smooth now.
The door doesn't stick.
The shelf doesn't tilt.

You sit back and look at it — this nothing thing that suddenly means everything.

Because for the first time in a long time,
you didn't abandon what you started.
You didn't give yourself an exit.
You stayed.

And in that staying, something else shifted.

Not loud.
Not grand.
But real.

You didn't fix your whole life.

You tightened one screw.

You lined up one edge.
You did one thing, all the way through.

And somehow — in some quiet, sacred way —
that's the beginning of a life that might stay steady too.

Pride in Silence

You don't tell anyone.

There's no photo.
No group chat update.
No journal entry with a gold star.

But something inside you sits a little taller today.

Not because the world noticed.
Because you did.

The trash was full — you took it out.
The sink had dishes — you cleaned them.
Your shirt was wrinkled — you changed it.

Tiny things.
Stupid, ordinary, invisible things.

But for someone who used to let everything slide,

these things are weight-bearing walls.

You don't text Chris.
You don't call your sister.
You don't even stand in front of the mirror practicing some dramatic monologue about how you're "turning it all around."

You just live today… like someone who respects themselves.
Quietly.
Unfolding that respect not in words,

but in action.

You walk past the cabinet — the one.
Still shut. Still holding.

And you don't pause this time.

Not because it's easy.
But because something deeper than fear or craving said, "Not today."
And you listened.

You go to bed with a clean sink.
A tired body.
And no one to applaud you.

But in the silence —
beneath the absence of noise or praise —
you feel something grow.

Pride.

Not the kind that demands to be seen.
The kind that lets you breathe in peace.

You don't say a word.
You just sleep.

And maybe for the first time in years…

you earned it.

PART IV
THE QUIET BECOMING

THE FEAR OF BEING OKAY

Waking Up Without Dread

You wake up.

And nothing hurts.

No pounding in your skull.
No bile in your throat.
No shame curling under your ribs like a warning.

Just… breath.

You lie still for a second, staring at the ceiling like it might crack and remind you who you were.

But it doesn't.

And that's when the fear starts.

Not the old fear.
Not the fear of falling apart.

But the fear that maybe…
you're okay.

And you don't know what to do with that.

Because chaos gave you purpose.
Regret gave you direction.

Pain gave you something to fight.

Now it's quiet.

And in the quiet —
a different kind of question whispers:

Who are you when you're not surviving?

You sit up.
Hands on knees.
Waiting for the weight to return.
The guilt. The hunger. The shake.

But it doesn't.

And that absence —
it feels more dangerous than the craving ever did.

You walk barefoot into the kitchen.
Pour coffee.
Toast bread.

It doesn't burn this time.

You catch your reflection in the window.

And the man there?
He's not broken.
He's not glowing either.
He's just... still.

You sip slowly.
Chew slowly.

And the silence isn't empty now.
It's full of things you've never had to face:

Peace.

Possibility.
The terrifying freedom of no longer being at war.

You stand there.

Not smiling.
Not weeping.
Just existing without armor.

And it's enough to shake something in you.

Not in fear.
But in awe.

Because maybe the scariest thing in recovery…
is not the pain you leave behind.

It's the quiet you learn to trust.

The Stillness Feels Wrong

You sit at the kitchen table.
No noise.
No movement.
No fight to win.
No mess to clean.

And somehow, it feels worse than the worst days.

Because stillness was never your natural state.
Chaos had a rhythm.
It gave your nervous system something to brace against.

This?
This is foreign.

You tap your fingers on the table.
One. Two. Three.

Waiting for something to break.

But nothing does.

There's no text from her.
No bottle calling from the cabinet.
No voice in your head shouting how worthless you are.

Just air.
Just light.
Just the hum of the fridge and the sound of your own breathing.

You check your phone.
No messages.
You open the cabinet — not for the bottle, just to check.

Still closed.

Still safe.

And yet your body stays tense.
As if something's wrong simply because nothing is.

Because for years, stillness meant the crash was coming.
The silence before the screaming.
The calm before you destroyed everything again.

So now, even peace feels like a setup.
Like it can't possibly be real.

And that's the war now.

Not against alcohol.
Not against the past.
But against the part of you that doesn't trust safety.

You sit back.
Let your spine touch the chair.

Let your hands rest.

Let the stillness stay, even if your mind doesn't know how.

And maybe this is the work now:

Learning how to live
in a world that no longer needs to be rescued from you.

Missing the Chaos

You don't want it back.
You swear you don't.
Not the bottles. Not the blackouts. Not the breaking things just to feel something.

But part of you—quiet, hidden—misses it.

Not the pain itself,
but the clarity it gave.

When you were drowning, at least you knew what to fight.
When everything was on fire, at least the smoke gave you direction.
When the world was loud, your own silence made more sense.

Now?

Now your life is… still.

Manageable.

You eat real food.
You wash your clothes.
You say "no" to the drink and "yes" to the coffee and "maybe" to the walk around the block.

And no one claps.
No one cries.

No one notices.

You used to be the problem everyone had to solve.
Now you're just a man folding laundry.

And it's good.
It is.

But you miss the edge.

The adrenaline.
The excuse.
The chaos that justified your collapse.

Because this quiet?
It doesn't give you an identity.
It doesn't tell you who you are.

It just asks you to figure that out—
without the fire,
without the mess,
without the crutches.

And that's harder than it sounds.

Because chaos gave you cover.
Now, peace gives you a mirror.

And the reflection?
It's steady.
But it's still forming.

And some days…
you'd rather be broken and certain
than whole and unsure.

But you don't reach for the match.
You don't light the fire.

You just sit with the ache of not needing it anymore.

And let that be the next kind of strength.

Letting Calm In

It doesn't knock.

Calm never does.

It shows up in strange ways —
in the smell of toast that doesn't burn,
in the mug that warms your hands without shaking,
in the quiet that doesn't feel like punishment.

At first, you treat it like a stranger.

You eye it with suspicion.

What does it want?
What is it hiding?

Because you've learned that stillness usually comes before the fall,
that silence was never peace, just the pause before yelling.
That soft moments were often the setup for collapse.

So when life goes quiet now, you flinch.

But this time…
nothing breaks.

You sip your coffee and no disaster follows.

You stand at the sink and no shame climbs your spine.

You sit on the couch and it doesn't swallow you whole.

And slowly — almost accidentally —
you realize this might be what safety feels like.

No highs.
No crashes.
Just breath.

You don't chase it away.

Not today.

You open the window.
Not for the drama of it. Just for the air.
And when the breeze brushes your skin,
you don't brace yourself.

You let it land.

You let it stay.

You let it in.

Because maybe calm was never the enemy.

Maybe you just didn't recognize it without the chaos around it.

And now —
you're learning.

Not how to fight.

But how to live
in the quiet you never trusted before.

THE FIRST REAL LAUGH

A Joke Over Coffee

It slips out.

Not a smile. Not a chuckle.
A real laugh.
Unexpected. Unguarded. Whole.

You're sitting at the table, coffee cooling in your hands.
Chris is standing at the counter, rambling about something — a neighbor, maybe, or that stupid squirrel that keeps finding ways into the trash.

He says something dumb.

Really dumb.

And without thinking, you laugh.

Sharp. Sudden. From the chest.

It catches you off guard.
Him too.

He glances over. Raises an eyebrow.
"You okay?"

You nod.
But you're not sure.

Because it's been so long since sound came out of you that wasn't pain, or apology, or defense.
So long since your ribs shook without it meaning you were breaking.

The laugh echoes a little too loud in the quiet kitchen.
But you don't walk it back.
You don't swallow it down.

You let it live.
Let it prove something.

Not that everything is fine.
Not that the past is gone.

But that joy —
even the smallest flicker of it —
can still find its way to the surface.

Even here.
Even now.
Even after everything.

And that?
That's worth noticing.

The Kid Laughs Too

You're not even hungry.

But you needed to be somewhere with people.

Somewhere where the light is warm, and the coffee isn't from your own machine. A place where the air hums with clinking cups and casual chatter. Noise that doesn't ask anything from you.

You take the corner table.

Order something simple — toast and a refillable cup of coffee.

You stare out the window. The world moves. Cars, clouds, lives.

And then you hear it.

A laugh.

Not just any laugh.

That kind of laugh that's so pure it cuts through noise like sunlight through blinds. High-pitched. Giddy. Untamed.

You look over.

Two tables down, a kid — maybe five — is squirming in his seat. His mom's trying to keep him still, but failing. And laughing too.

He's got a crayon in each hand and syrup on his face, and he says something you don't catch — but she bursts out laughing like she wasn't expecting to feel that happy this early in the day.

You freeze.

Because for one second, it feels like the whole café softens. Like something cracked open and let some light in.

The boy leans over, whispers something else, and she laughs again — that kind of laugh people don't fake. The kind that's built from love and exhaustion and a morning that hasn't broken yet.

Your chest tightens.

But not in pain.

In memory.

In longing.

In that ache that says: *you've known this once.*

Not envy.

Not regret.

Just the kind of quiet reminder that joy still exists in the world — and it doesn't always have to come from you to matter.

You sip your coffee.

It's bitter.

But for some reason, it doesn't taste empty.

You don't stare too long. You don't intrude.

But you feel it.

Something shifts.

Something loosens.

And when the boy catches your eye — just for a second — he grins, sticky and wild, like you're just another safe grown-up in a kind-enough world.

You nod.

And when you leave a little later, your steps feel lighter.

Not healed.

Not whole.

But human. Again.

Joy Doesn't Ask Permission

It just shows up.

Not when you're ready.
Not when you've earned it.

Not when everything's fixed.

Just… now.

You're walking down the sidewalk, paper coffee cup in hand. The sky's overcast but not angry. The kind of grey that makes colors feel louder.

You pass a storefront — small, local. Smells like warm bread and cinnamon. There's a family inside. A little girl presses her face to the glass, fogging it with her breath, then draws a crooked heart with her fingertip. Her dad laughs. Her mom rolls her eyes and tousles the girl's hair.

You smile. You don't mean to.
You just do.

Not a big one. Not performative.
Just a flicker of something soft at the corners of your mouth.

It doesn't last long.
But it lands.

Joy didn't knock.
Didn't ask if you were still broken.
Didn't care about your past or your last relapse or how long it's been since you said, "I'm fine," and meant it.

It just arrived.
Like a breath you didn't realize you'd been holding.

And when you keep walking, something is lighter.
Not everything. Not yet.
But enough.

Enough to not look down at your shoes.
Enough to feel your own heartbeat.

Enough to take another sip of coffee — this time actually tasting it.

Joy doesn't ask permission.
It just shows up.

And maybe for the first time in years —
you let it.

"I Forgot I Could Feel This"

It hits you in the smallest moment.

You're sitting on a bench outside the café, sun warming your forearms, not too hot. Just enough to remind your skin what soft feels like.

You're not thinking about yesterday.

You're not panicking about tomorrow.

You're just… here.

And then it comes.

A feeling.

Not loud. Not sharp.
Not even easy to name.
But real.

A lift in your chest. A stretch behind your ribs. Like a window opened in a house you forgot had them.

It's not joy, exactly.
Not relief either.
It's the absence of armor.
The pause between defenses.

The simple fact of being alive… and not wanting to run from it.

You look up.

A couple walks past, holding hands. She says something you can't hear, and he laughs — not polite, but full. The kind that leans into trust.

And you smile.
Not at them.
Just… to yourself.

"I forgot I could feel this," you think.

This quiet, grounded okay-ness.
This small pulse of hope that doesn't beg to be bigger.
This moment that isn't haunted by the next one.

Your coffee's cold now.
You don't mind.

You sit there longer than you planned.
Not because you're avoiding anything.
But because, for once, you're not chasing anything either.

And that?

That's the kind of peace you never thought you'd get to feel without earning it in pain.

But here it is anyway.

Unannounced.
Undeserved.
Unmistakably yours.

THE SMALLEST BRAVE THING

The Bottle in the Cabinet

You pass it again.

That cabinet.

The one you haven't opened in weeks.

You could tell someone it doesn't bother you anymore.
That you've moved past it.
But that would be a lie.
A quieter one, maybe — but still a lie.

Because it's still there.

That bottle.

Tucked behind the old tea bags and a box of stale crackers.
Wrapped in the kind of silence that doesn't need words to scream.

You stand there, hand resting on the counter.
Not touching the handle.
Just… listening.

To the thoughts that still know your name.

It doesn't call to you like it used to.
But it doesn't disappear either.
It waits.

Not because it's powerful.
Because it's patient.

You breathe.

Not a big, heroic inhale.
Just enough to steady your hand.
Just enough to stay with yourself.

You glance around.

No audience.
No spotlight.
No one to see what you're about to do — or not do.

And maybe that's why it matters more.

Because the hardest bravery
is the kind no one claps for.

You stay still.

Long enough to feel the craving curl up and shrink.
Long enough to hear your own voice — faint but firm — say:

"Not today."

You walk away.

Not because you conquered it.

But because you didn't obey it.

And that's the smallest brave thing you can do.

But damn if it doesn't feel like the beginning of something bigger.

One Breath, One Bag

It doesn't start with a grand moment.

No music.
No speech.
No vision of your future self holding a 30-day chip in front of a cheering crowd.

It starts with standing in front of the cabinet.

Again.

Same as yesterday.
Same as the day before.

Only today, something's... different.
Not stronger. Not braver. Just... still.

You stare at the door.
Not like a man resisting temptation.
Like a man deciding what story he doesn't want to tell anymore.

You breathe in.
Not deep. Just enough.
Enough to keep your hand steady.

And you open the drawer — the one with the trash bags.

Pull one out.

The sound is soft. Plastic against plastic.
But in your chest, it booms like a drum.

You walk back to the cabinet.
Open it.

You don't hesitate.

You just move.

Not fast. Not dramatic.
Like a man taking out spoiled food.

Like something that once served a purpose, but now only carries weight.

The bottle is heavier than it should be.
Like it knows.

You place it in the bag.
Then another.
Then the half-full one with the sticky cap and the label peeling off.

The bag sags.

You tie it shut.
Double knot.

And for a moment, you just… stand there.
One hand on the knot.
One foot slightly back.
Like if someone walked in right now, they'd think this was no big deal.

But it is.

It's the weight of every "I'll quit tomorrow."
Every "just one more."
Every promise you broke — to yourself, to them, to the man in the mirror.

All knotted up in plastic.

You lift it.
And it doesn't fight.

You carry it to the door.

The morning light peeks through the blinds — golden, soft, indifferent.
Like the world kept moving while you were frozen.

And now, it's offering you a moment to catch up.

You open the front door.

Step out.

The air hits you — sharp but clean.

You walk to the bin.
Lift the lid.
Drop the bag.

It lands with a dull thud.

And something in you exhales — not just air, but years.
Of hiding.
Of circling.
Of surviving.

You turn back toward the house.

And this time,
you don't carry the weight with you.

You just carry the man who finally let go.

And that's enough.

Throwing It Out

The bag is gone.

Not sitting by the door.
Not waiting in the hallway like a dare.
Not heavy in your hand like it was holding you back.

Gone.

And you're standing in the kitchen,

hands on the counter,
still bracing for some kind of aftershock.

But it doesn't come.

No regret.
No rush to undo it.
No panic chasing you back out the door.

Just… quiet.

An empty cabinet.
A trash bin halfway down the block holding what used to be your exit.
And a silence that doesn't ache.

You walk through the house.
Touch the edge of the couch.
Straighten a frame that's been tilted for months.
Not because it matters —
but because you finally noticed.

You open the fridge.
Pour a glass of water.
The kind of plain act you never thought twice about.

But today, it feels like an oath.
To stay.
To feel.
To live — even when it's unremarkable.

You sit at the table.
Sip slowly.
No trembling.
No flinching.

Just presence.

You're not chasing something.
You're not numbing something.
You're just here.

And that?

That's the miracle no one applauds.

No finish line.
No speech.

Just a man,
in a quiet house,
drinking water —
because he finally believes he's allowed to stay.

Empty Cabinet, Full Chest

You open it without thinking.

Just habit.

The cabinet where the bottles used to be.

For a second, your brain fills in the missing shapes — the labels, the glass, the quiet lies they used to tell.

But it's empty.

Utterly, beautifully empty.

Not reorganized.
Not repurposed.
Just… space.

Your hand hovers inside. Not reaching. Just noticing.

There's nothing to grab. Nothing to hide.
Nothing to fight against.

And your chest, unexpectedly, fills.

Not with pride.
Not with victory.
With **room**.

Like your ribs remembered they were built for breathing, not bracing.

You stand there a moment longer.

Long enough to realize the absence doesn't scare you.

It frees you.

Because emptiness isn't always a loss.

Sometimes it's the beginning of something else:
A place to store what matters.
A place to let stillness settle.
A place where cravings used to live — now ready for peace.

You close the door.

It doesn't creak.

It doesn't resist.

It just closes — like it's been waiting for this chapter to end.

And inside your chest?

Not glass.
Not guilt.
Not noise.

Just the quiet, steady weight of someone finally giving themselves permission to breathe fully.

Not to be better.

Just to be here.
And that's enough.

For now...
that's more than enough.

PART V
THE MAN WHO CAME BACK

BRIDGES, NOT APOLOGIES

A Call to the Woman Who Raised Him

You stare at the phone like it's something fragile.
Like it might shatter if you press the wrong button.
Like it might shatter you.

The contact's still saved.
You never deleted it.
Just moved it lower and lower in your mind — under guilt, under time, under silence.

You sit at the table.
The same one you fixed last week.
The surface still leans slightly left, but it holds your elbows. Your weight. Your fear.

You breathe once.
Twice.
Then press "Call."

It rings.

And in those seconds, it all rushes in —
her hands fixing your collar on the first day of school,
the night you called her a name you've never said to anyone else,
the voicemail you never returned,
the birthday you forgot,

the time she said, "I'm scared for you," and you laughed like she was overreacting.

You feel your throat tighten.

You could hang up.

You almost do.

But the line clicks.

Not her voice — just the beep.

Voicemail.

And suddenly, that's worse.
Because now it's all on you.

You open your mouth.

Nothing comes.

You grip the phone tighter, like you can wring words from your fingers.

Then, somehow, they come.

"Hey… it's me."

Your voice sounds too small. Too late.

"I know we haven't talked. I know I should've…"

You stop.

Start again.

"I don't know what to say. But I needed to try."

You feel it now — the tears. Not loud. Not falling. Just *there*.
Like a weight behind your ribs.

You wipe your cheek.

"I just… I wanted you to know I'm still here."

Silence.

And for now — that's all you can say.

You hang up.

Not because it's finished.
But because something inside you finally started.

"I Don't Need You to Forgive Me"

The next day, she calls back.

You don't answer right away.

You watch the phone ring — name glowing on the screen like a question you're not sure how to solve.

But your thumb moves anyway.

You pick up.

Silence.

Then her breath.

"Hey."

That voice — older, softer. But still hers.

You sit down. Because standing feels like too much.

"Hi," you say. Almost whisper it.

Another pause.

Then:

"I got your message."

You nod, even though she can't see you.

"Yeah," you say. "I didn't really know what I was trying to say."

More silence. But not the kind that hurts.

You exhale.

"I'm not calling to make anything right," you say. "I just… wanted you to hear it from me. That I know I disappeared. That I left you with all the fear and none of the answers."

She doesn't interrupt.

You keep going.

"And I'm not asking you to forgive me."

You pause.

"Because I don't need you to."

That part surprises even you.

"I mean—don't get me wrong—God, it would mean the world. But this time… I'm not trying to fix it with words. I just wanted you to know I see it now. I see what I did. And I'm sorry. But not because I want something back. Just… because it's true."

There's a sound on the other end. Like a breath breaking. Or a heart unlocking.

Silence.

Then — from the other end of the line — a sound.

Not a word.

Just… quiet crying.

The kind someone tries to hide but can't.

You press the phone tighter to your ear.

Then, through the tears — her voice. Barely above a whisper.

"I'm just glad you're alive."

That's it.

No lecture.

No dramatic welcome.

Just that.

And that's enough.

Because this time, you didn't beg for a reset.

You didn't cover your guilt with flowers or future promises.

You just showed up.

You stood still.

And on the other end of the line…

so did she.

Silence That Didn't Hurt

The call ends,
but the sound of her voice lingers.

You sit for a while,
phone still in your hand,
like maybe the connection isn't gone yet.

There's no flood of relief.
No dramatic music.

Just… stillness.

But it's a different kind of stillness.

Not the lonely kind.
Not the "why didn't I say more" kind.
It's softer. Warmer.
Like standing on a bridge that hasn't fallen.

The next morning, you don't expect anything.
You're not waiting.
But when your phone buzzes —
just a photo.
A sunrise through her kitchen window.

No caption.

And that's everything.

You stare at it longer than you should.
Not because the sky is pretty.
But because she shared it with *you*.

No explanations.
No pressure.
Just a small thread, held out.

A few days pass.
Then you send a picture back.
The mug you used to drink from in her house.
Cracked, but still holding warmth.

She replies with a heart.

It's not fast.
Not loud.
Not healed.

But it's not broken either.

And slowly —
the silence shifts.

Still there.
But no longer heavy.

No longer punishment.
No longer proof of distance.

Now it's just space.
Room for something to grow.

Something that might not need to be named.
Not yet.
Maybe not ever.

But when you sit down again,
when the room is quiet,
you don't fear the stillness.

You recognize it.

And for the first time in years —
it doesn't hurt.

It holds.

WHAT HE CAME BACK FOR

The Walk to the Playground

You spot him before he sees you.

Same park. Same bench. Same rusted swing set.
He's older now. Taller.
Shoes too clean — someone's taking care of him.

He's sitting alone.
Backpack beside him. Elbows on knees.
Watching the other kids like he's not sure how to join them.

You hesitate.
It feels like a hundred miles from the sidewalk to that bench.

But you walk.
Slow. No rehearsed speech.
Just the weight of every missed birthday in your chest.

You stop a few feet away.

He looks up.

His face doesn't change much.
No anger. No smile.
Just… recognition.
Like seeing someone you used to know in a dream.

You sit on the edge of the bench.

Not close. Not far.

He doesn't move.
You don't push.

You just say it.

"Hey."

A beat.
Then — his quiet: "Hey."

Silence. The good kind. The earned kind.

And then — you breathe in, feel your voice shake, and say:
"I'm sorry."
He looks at you.

"For not being there," you add.
"When it mattered most. For not being the dad you deserved."

His eyes stay on yours.
Still no reaction.
And you think — maybe that's it. Maybe this is all.

But then…
he says:

"Why now?"

You answer with the only truth you have:

"Because I finally became someone who could walk here without lying to you."

Another pause.

Then — you shift.
Turn toward him.

And open your arms — not wide. Not dramatic.

Just… open.

He doesn't move at first.

But then, like something cracked and let go —
he leans in.

You feel his arms wrap around you — tight, like he was holding it in for years.
You wrap yours around him.
Feel the weight of everything that never got said.

And somewhere in the middle of that quiet, heavy hug —
you feel it.

Wet. On your cheek.
And his.

No one else is watching.
Just two sets of arms.
Two sets of tears.

And a second that rewrites a hundred yesterdays.

Two Sets of Eyes

You don't speak right away.

Not because there's nothing to say.

But because the words would crack the moment open too wide —
and neither of you is ready for that just yet.

So you sit.

Beside him.

Same bench.

Same air.

Different people.

He kicks his shoes against the dirt. Not restless. Just… present.

You glance sideways.
He's older than your memory wants him to be.
Longer legs. Narrower face.
A quiet confidence that didn't come from you —
and somehow that's the hardest part.

He doesn't look at you.

Not at first.

But then, as if something pulls his gaze,
he lifts his chin and finds your eyes.

And you look back.

No flinch.

No turn-away.

No fake smile.

Just two sets of eyes,
trying to read pages that were never written —
because someone put the pen down too soon.

You don't know what he sees in you.

Exhaustion? Regret? Hope?

But what you see in him…
is everything you missed.

The scraped knees you didn't bandage.
The drawings you didn't pin to the fridge.
The bedtime stories left unread.

And still —
he doesn't look away.

He sees you.

Not the version you practiced in the mirror.
Not the man you hoped to be.

Just… you.

And for the first time, that feels like enough.

You clear your throat.

He doesn't speak.

But he doesn't leave either.

You both just sit there.

Two sets of eyes.

One quiet beginning.

The Hug That Said Everything

You don't expect anything more.

The bench already gave you more than you thought you deserved.
A seat beside him.
A shared silence.
A single "Hey."

But then he shifts.

Not much — just a subtle lean in your direction.

Like a plant turning toward light.

You don't speak.

Words would only fumble here,
try to control what needs to happen on its own.

Then his hand — small, still unsure — brushes yours on the bench.
Not grabbing.
Just… touching.
Like a question with no punctuation.

You turn your palm upward.

Let it be an answer.

He slips his hand into yours.

And you freeze — not from fear, but reverence.
Because this — this is the moment.
Not loud.
Not scripted.

A boy reaching toward a father
who finally stopped disappearing.

You don't say, "Thank you."

You don't say, "I love you."

You don't say anything.

You just pull him — gently —
into the space between grief and grace.

And he lets you.

His head against your chest.

Your arms around him.

No sobs.

Just breathing.

A rhythm that says:
We both broke.
But we're here now.

His fingers grip the back of your shirt.
Not hard.
But enough to say:

Don't let go too fast.

And you won't.

Because this isn't forgiveness.

This isn't forgetting.

This is something quieter.
Older.
Deeper.

This is **the hug that said everything**.
Without saying a word.

"You Can Come Home If You Want"

You don't plan to say it.

You never rehearsed it.

It wasn't part of some imaginary script about how this moment should go.

But as you sit there—

your son's head still leaning on your shoulder,

his fingers still curled in the fabric of your shirt like he's afraid it might vanish again—

you feel something loosen in your chest.

Not pain.

Not guilt.

Just the thing that lives underneath them both.

Love.

The kind that doesn't ask for permission.

The kind that keeps showing up long after the damage has been done.

You look down at him.

And he looks up at you.

Eyes a little red.

Breath catching just slightly,
like he doesn't trust this moment to stay.

You clear your throat.

Not to be strong.

Just to make space for the words that need to live outside your body.

And then—

quietly, like handing him something fragile—

you say:

"You can come home, if you want."

He doesn't answer.

Not with words.

But his face shifts.

That flicker of disbelief.
That moment of *is this real?*

And then he nods.

Just once.

Not dramatic.

But honest.

And in that nod, something inside you breaks.
Not apart—
open.

Because you never knew
how much hope could live
in seven words.

Because you thought you were offering him something.

But what you didn't expect
was what he gave back.

A second chance.

A crack of light in a life that had gone dim.

You pull him a little closer.

And for the first time in a long, long time—

you feel it, deep in your bones:

You didn't just come to the playground.

You came back
to your life.

And someone
was still waiting for you
when you arrived.

THIS ISN'T THE END.
IT'S THE BEGINNING
OF SOMEONE ELSE'S STORY —
BECAUSE OF YOU

You made it here.

Maybe you read every page.
Maybe you stopped and started.
Maybe you skipped chapters, came back later, sat in silence with just one sentence that landed harder than you expected.

However you got here —
you showed up.

And that matters.

I don't know what's changed in your life since page one.
Maybe a little.
Maybe a lot.
Maybe nothing on the outside yet, but something deep inside you has started to move.

Maybe you took one breath when you would've run.
Maybe you deleted one number.
Maybe you said "I'm sorry" and meant it.
Maybe… you just didn't drink today.

And maybe — that's enough.

Whatever shifted, whatever stayed with you —
I hope it gave you one small thing:
the reminder that it's not too late.

And now?

Now, you get the chance to do something quietly powerful.

Leave a review.
Not for me.
For the next person.

The one who's where you were —
scrolling through titles, not sure if anything can still reach them.

Your words might be the reason they pause.
The reason they say,
"Maybe this one will understand me."

You don't have to write a novel.
You don't have to say anything fancy.

Just honest.

Because your voice might be the bridge between someone else's pain and their first step toward healing.

And that?

That's something real.

Thank you for being here.
Thank you for reading.
Thank you — if you choose — to speak.

Because sometimes,
your words are the ones someone else has been waiting to hear.

Published by AK Media Publishing

Copyright © 2025 by Ben Mallory
All rights reserved.

No part of this publication may be reproduced, stored in a retrieval system, or transmitted in any form or by any means—electronic, mechanical, photocopying, recording, or otherwise—without the prior written permission of the publisher.

ISBN: 978-3-911943-01-7
Printed and distributed by PublishDrive
www.publishdrive.com

Ben Mallory is represented by:
Artur Kolmai
Krambergstr. 11c
58099 Hagen
Germany

Disclaimer: This book is intended for informational and inspirational purposes only. It reflects the author's personal experiences, opinions, and interpretations. It is not a substitute for professional advice, diagnosis, or treatment. Readers should consult qualified professionals regarding individual situations. The author and publisher assume no liability for the use or misuse of the content.

www.ingramcontent.com/pod-product-compliance
Lightning Source LLC
Chambersburg PA
CBHW061536231125
35807CB00032B/161